CHICAGO
AMERICA'S WORKSHOP

PETER N. PERO

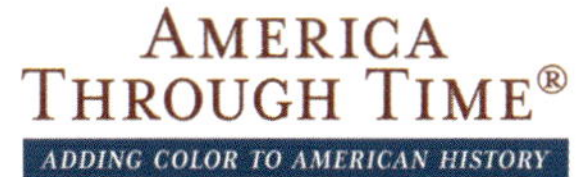

America Through Time is an imprint of Fonthill Media LLC
www.through-time.com
office@through-time.com

Published by Arcadia Publishing by arrangement with Fonthill Media LLC
For all general information, please contact Arcadia Publishing:
Telephone: 843-853-2070
Fax: 843-853-0044
E-mail: sales@arcadiapublishing.com
For customer service and orders:
Toll-Free 1-888-313-2665

www.arcadiapublishing.com

First published 2021

ISBN 978-1-63499-313-5

Typeset in Mrs Eaves XL Serif Narrow
Printed and bound in England

CONTENTS

Introduction

Chicago has long been a powerful workshop to the world. For more than a century, the city nurtured thousands of companies that supplied a hungry nation with industrial products. Manufacturers with core brands that survived many decades are featured inside this book.

This survey identifies factors that sustained Chicago's economic growth: favorable geography, mass marketing, and a knack for invention are positive factors. Influences leading to economic decline are shortsighted planning, cut-throat competition, and slow technologic growth.

This book does not have the space to survey numerous small businesses. Many thrived in Chicago, but only large firms that served a national market are at the heart of this book. The large companies in this study were "born and raised" in Chicago and continued production for more than fifty years.

Industrial Landscape

In the late 1800s, large industrial sites were situated along the banks of the Chicago River and the shoreline of Lake Michigan. A vital confluence of railways, highways, and airways contributed to the city's phenomenal growth. From the 1960s to the present, two international airports and a vital interstate auto network continued to churn commercial traffic.

The Human Element

Creativity and capital helped hundreds of large industries to grow. Furthermore, many thousands of immigrants and local artisans supplied the city with robust labor. Over time, millions of customers, brought enormous profits to large Chicago manufacturers.

Rich Resources

An abundant supply of lumber and metals helped energize tool making, bridge building, home construction, and furniture production in Early Chicago. With the growth of these industries came good paying jobs. Austin Weber, who authored *Made in Chicago,* on the growth of manufacturing wrote, "Thousands who worked on assembly lines, and in foundries or machine shops in Chicago earned steady pay that led to home ownership and even a college education." Workers with lunch boxes and briefcases contributed to the growth of Chicago industry and made the city an economic powerhouse.

New Horizons

Heavy industry is no longer the backbone of Chicago's economy. Many businesses featured in this book were the victims of financial mergers, hostile takeovers, or closures. The technology revolution that now fuels Chicago does not depend on oil, metal, or smoke. Instead, the city has created a new reputation based on high quality services: Arthur Anderson for accounting, Leo Burnett in advertising, Allstate for insurance, and Skidmore Owings and Merrill for architecture. These are examples of renowned white-collar companies that have reached international heights. Today, Chicago holds rank in the post-industrial world. Motorola, Boeing, and Abbott Labs are examples of city corporations known across the nation and most of the world. The city now attracts international investors for its products, plants and local workforce. This combination will help shape the economic history of Chicago for another century to come.

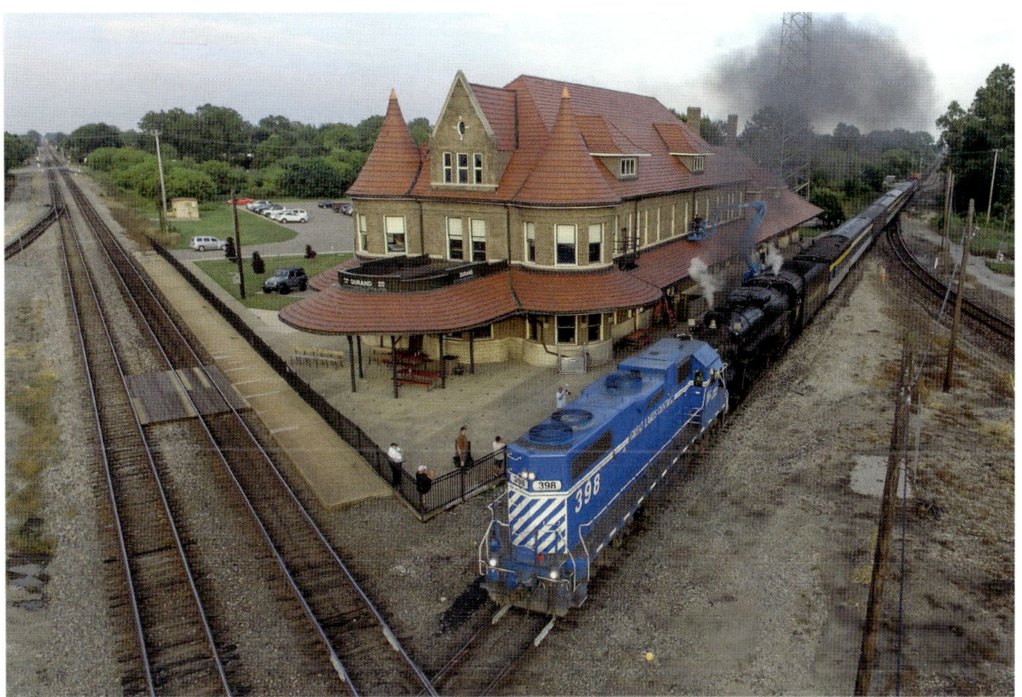

1

HEAVY INDUSTRY

For many decades, Chicago was a center for heavy industry. Regarding the steel industry, the city was a world leader. In addition to iron ore, there were Great Lakes ports for hauling raw material and for shipping the final products. Property was low priced, and a huge immigrant work force was readily available.

From 1875 to 1975, a parade of mills operated on low-cost lakefront land. The Inland Steel Company, Republic Steel Inc., Iroquois Steel, Wisconsin Steel Inc., and Youngstown Steel were all prosperous mills on the border of Illinois and Indiana. At its high point, all the mills together employed nearly 50,000 workers. One of the most prosperous was Ryerson Steel Company. Joseph T. Ryerson teamed up with Henry Ford for automotive production—when Ford produced new cars, Ryerson produced new wheels.

Today, a small number of steel mills still exist in the South Chicago area. The U.S. Steel Corporation and Arcelor-Mittal Co. are key metal producers. The Ryerson Co. still has its headquarters in Chicago with subsidiaries across the USA and in Canada. Arcelor-Mittal is a Brazilian-Indian conglomerate. The steel business in Chicago now relies on offshore partners, plus overseas customers, in order to stay in business. The solution for the American steel industry, during the Trump era, was to tariff and tax steel created by overseas competitors.

Cyrus McCormick's Reaper Company first opened in 1847, as a solution for farmers to harvest acres of crops in a single day. Later called International Harvester, the company made tractors for a worldwide market. Today, the company still relies on the export business and calls itself the Navistar Corporation. It produces railroad cars, buses, and mass transit (green vehicles).

For decades, Chicago was a meatpacker to the world. The city of "the big shoulders" was a major railroad hub, and huge firms such as Armour Inc. and the Swift Company were negligent regarding meat inspection and work safety. The dangers of their industry were exposed in 1907 by muckraking journalist, Upton Sinclair, and eventually regulated by federal law.

Another controversial company on Chicago's Southside was the Pullman Corp. In addition to the railroad car factory, George Pullman experimented with housing and community planning schemes. Pullman's Palace Car Company began in 1867, as a kind of hotel on wheels. With hundreds of acres of open prairie, the industrialist and patriarch built rental apartments for his workers, rowhouses for the managers, and even a church for his favorite denomination. At its peak, Mr. Pullman employed nearly 10,000 workers, but by 1894, a massive strike rocked the company and Pullman's dream for creating an industrial utopia failed.

The "go-go years" of Chicago industry became sluggish by the 1970s. The International Harvester Corporation closed its plant by 1972. The Zenith Television Corporation shuttered by 1977. The Schwinn Company stopped making bicycles in Chicago by 1984, and Western Electric Company morphed into AT&T by 1983. Many more small manufacturers fell prey to mergers, buy-outs, or bankruptcy while many Chicago factories moved to Latin America and Asia to take advantage of low cost labor. Chicago Industry needed to retool, redesign, and reinvest itself. (For a summary of how Chicago industries survived the business recession of the 1980s, read the introductory chapter in this book.)

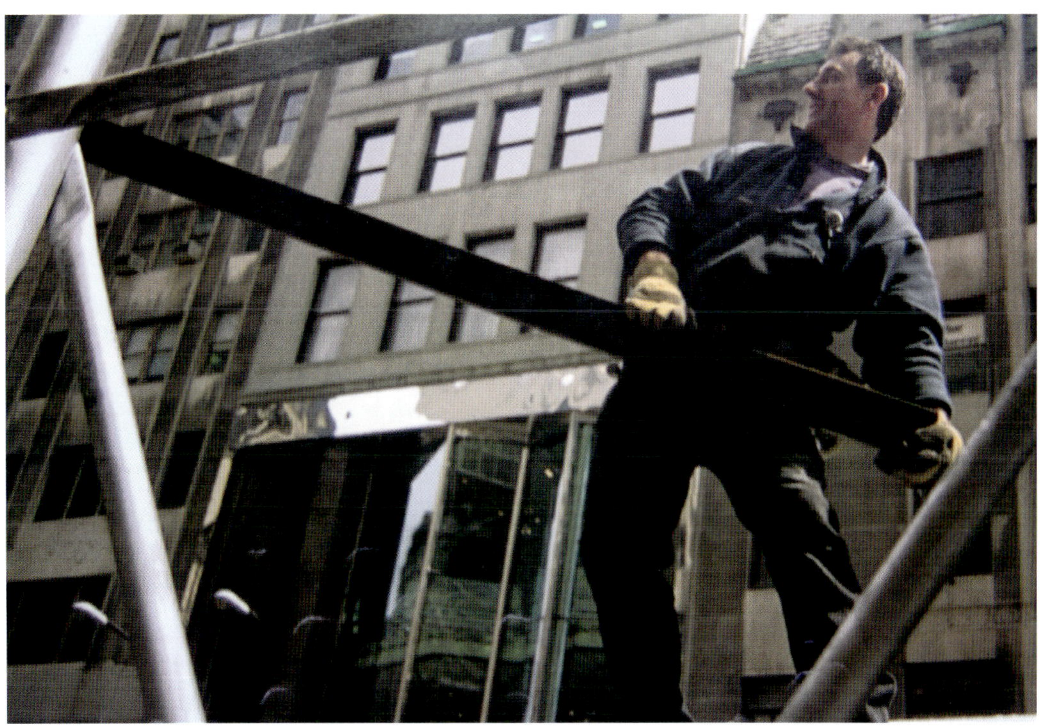

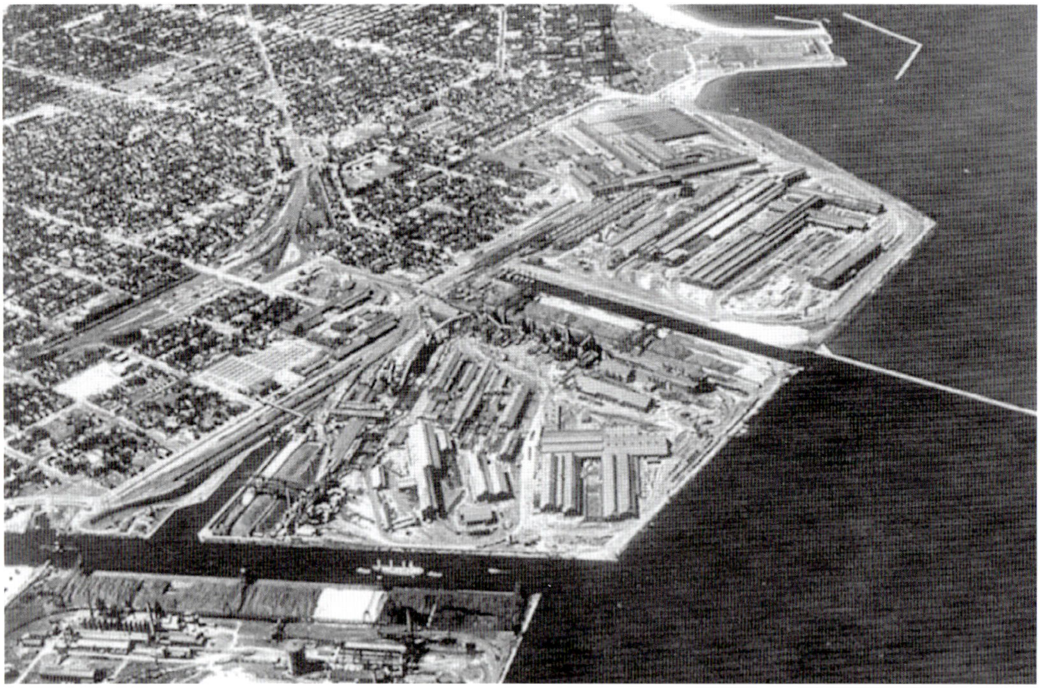

Village of Steel: Steel factories covered acres of lakefront land from South Chicago to the Indiana border. Lake Michigan provided coolant for molten steel, plus convenient passage for shipping byproducts. For decades, the steel industry created thousands of jobs, but also pollution problems for the companies and the surrounding neighborhood. Here, three men handle a shipload of galvanized piping.

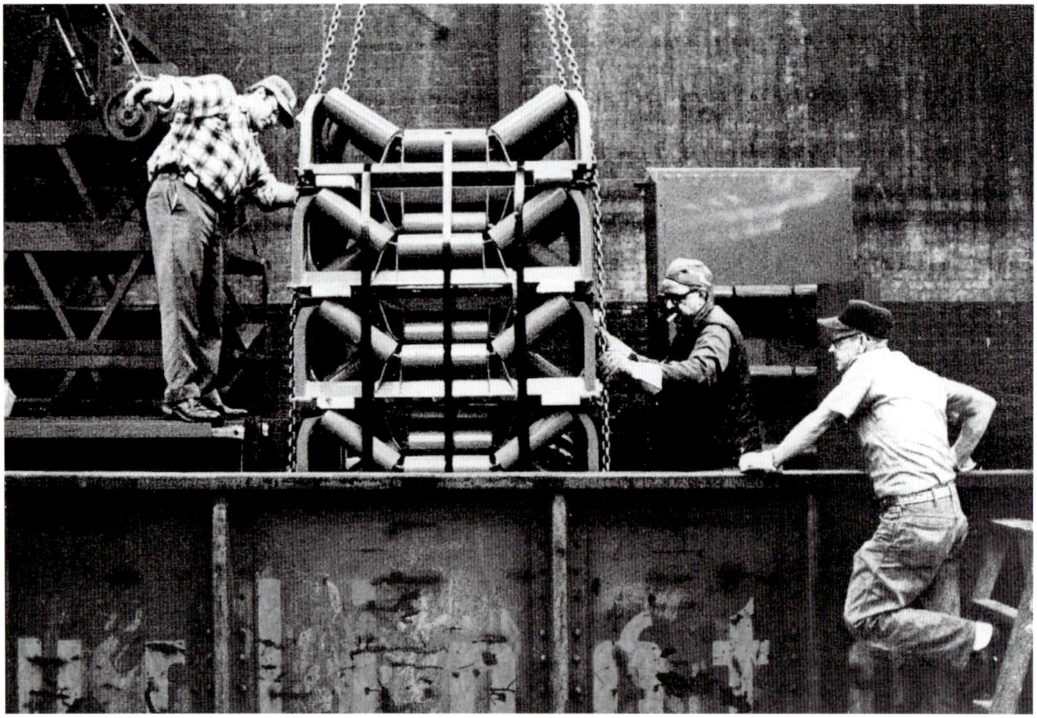

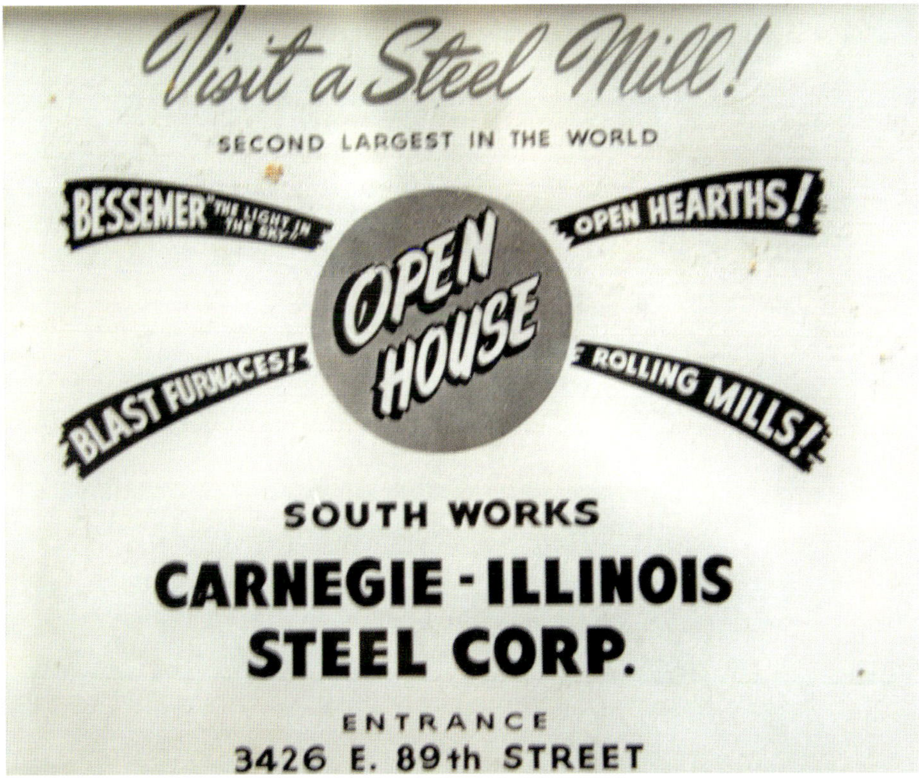

Visit a Steel Mill!

SECOND LARGEST IN THE WORLD

BESSEMER "THE LIGHT IN THE SKY!"

OPEN HEARTHS!

OPEN HOUSE

BLAST FURNACES!

ROLLING MILLS!

SOUTH WORKS

CARNEGIE - ILLINOIS
STEEL CORP.

ENTRANCE
3426 E. 89th STREET

SURVIVING THE CRITICS: In an effort to counter public criticism, the steel mills offered "Open House" days for tourists and guests. A day at the blast furnace lured students, neighbors, and curiosity seekers to witness hot-rolled steel in the making. In addition to the tours, one company organized a popular band to assuage workers by offering entertainment at the mill.

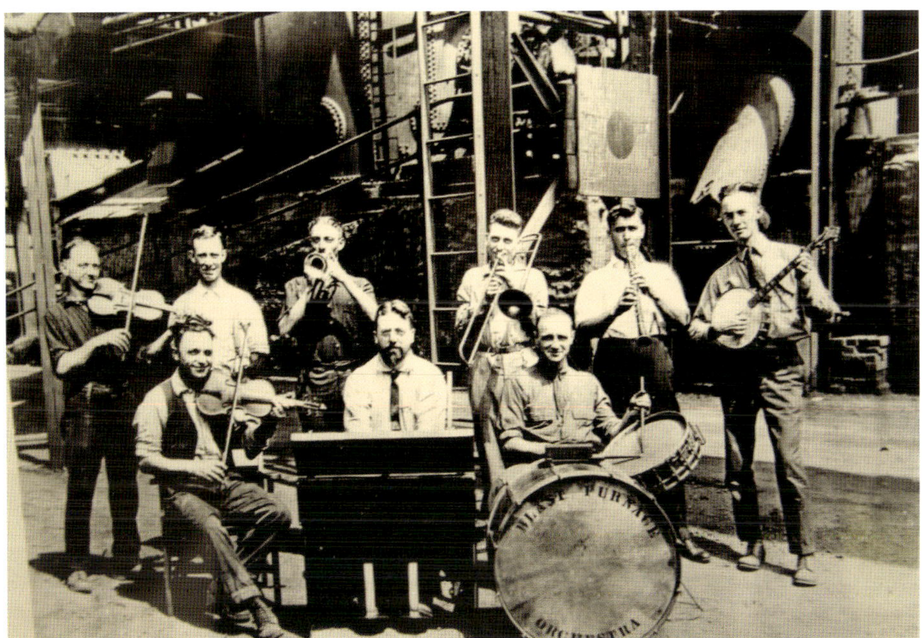

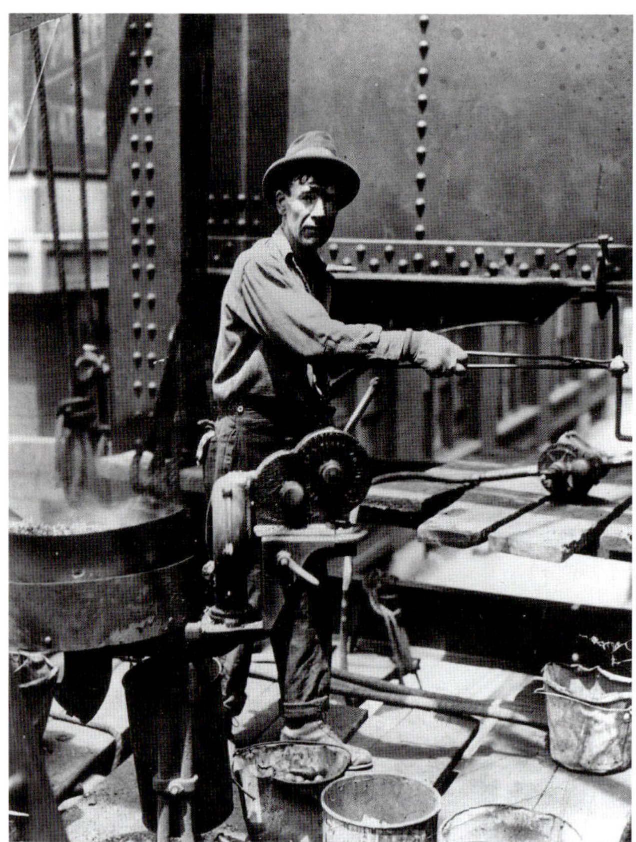

LABOR CONFLICTS: Working conditions worsened in the mills. Steel workers wanted to create a union for promoting better wages and a safer environment. By the 1930s, seven steel companies were prospering in Chicago, but labor and management fought bitterly. During a Memorial Day picnic, private police security opened fire at union families in a riot that killed ten men; seven of them were shot in the back.

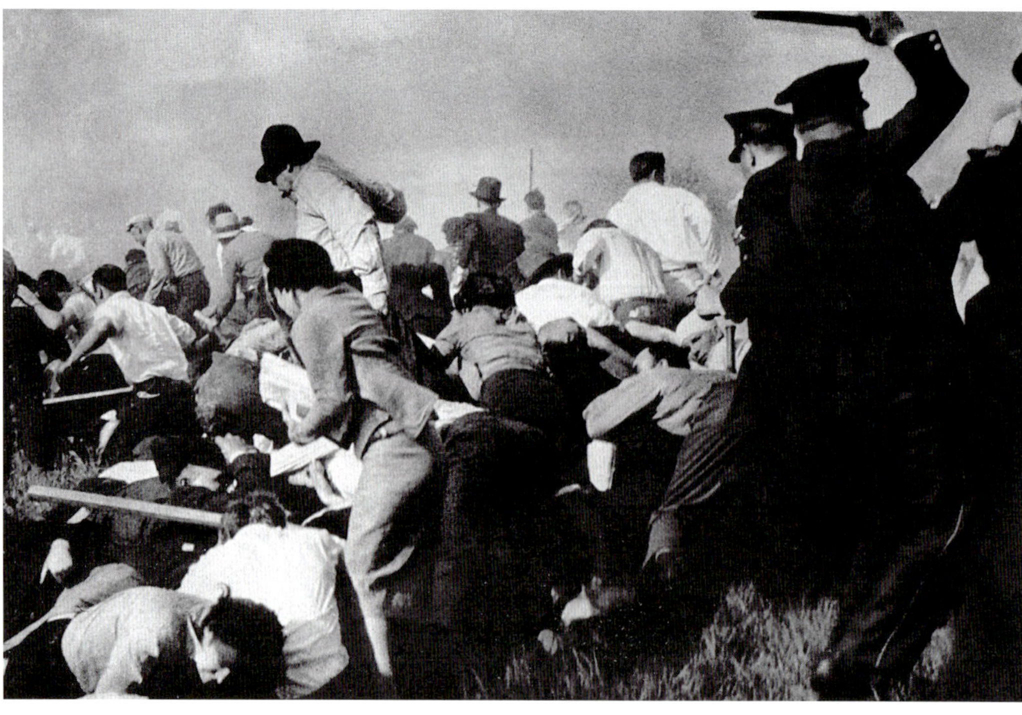

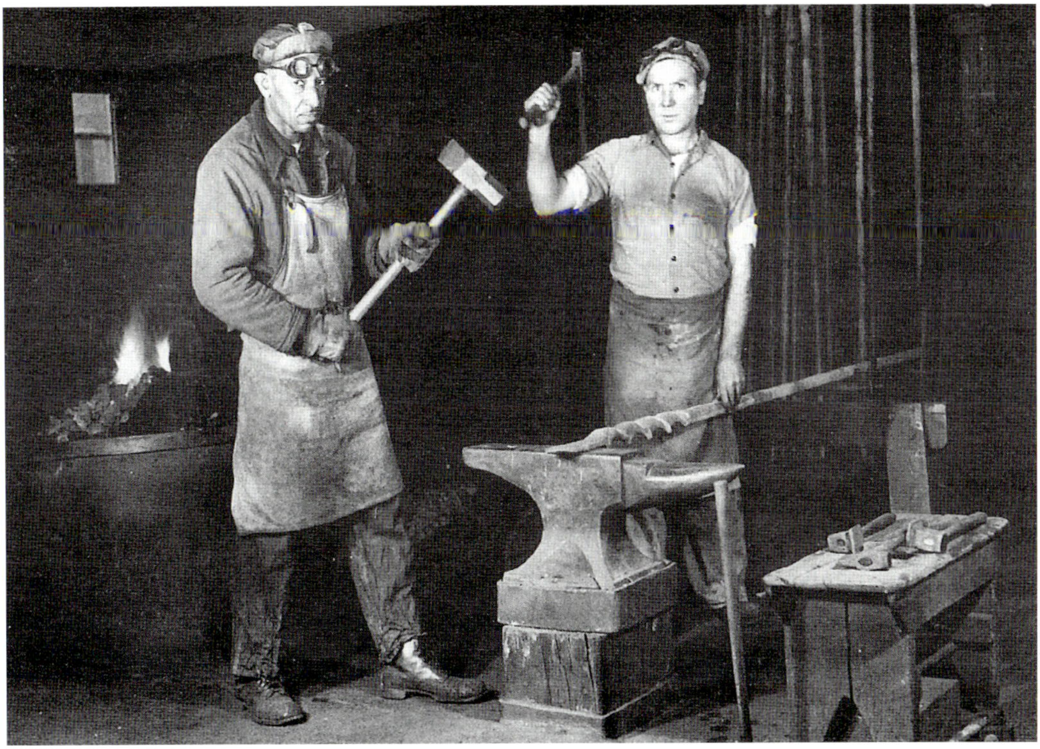

COMPETITIVE LABOR: Many immigrant steel workers applied their skills on the job. Today, their descendants continue to produce iron, stainless steel, and a number of hybrid alloys. The United States Steel Corporation remains as the largest operation on the Southside today. Chicago firms must export steel to survive. This task is challenging since overseas steel makers are now establishing their own plants in Chicago.

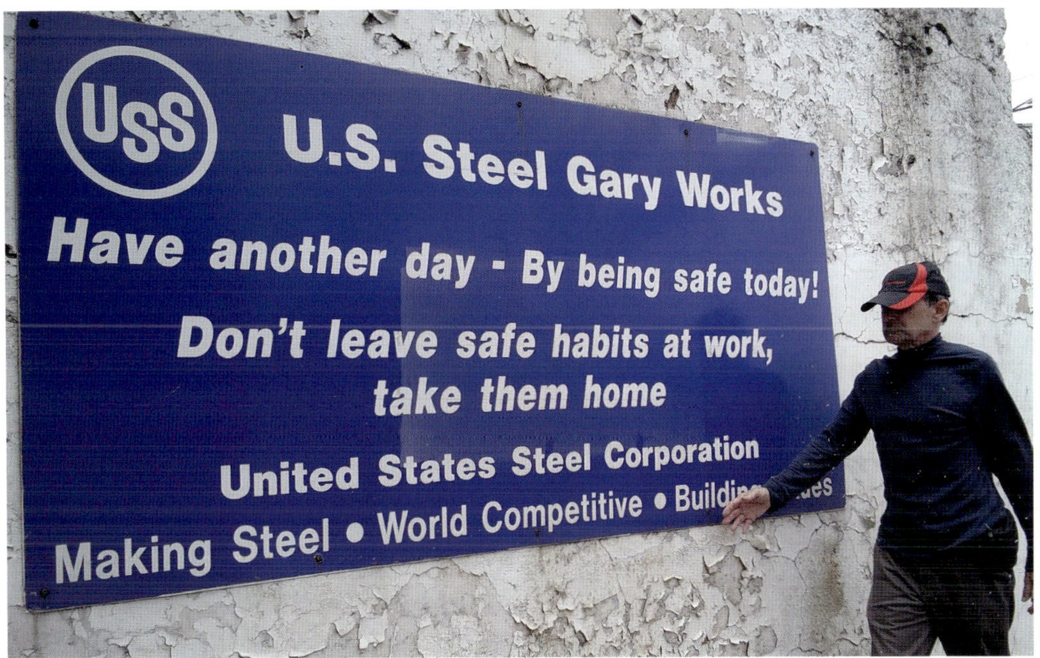

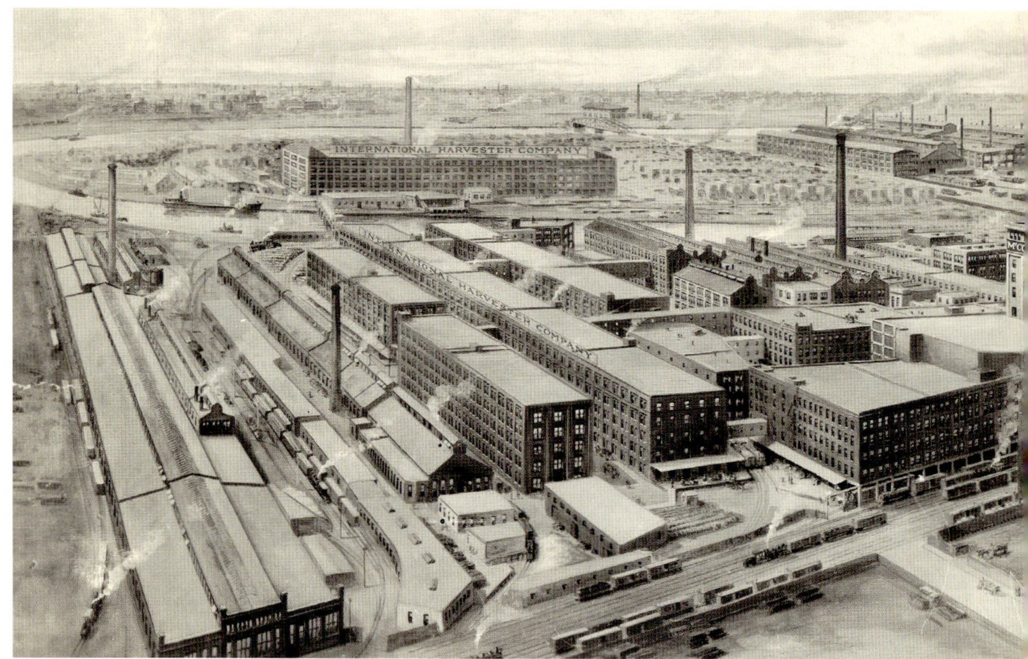

ACRES OF WORK: International Harvester occupied acres of city blocks, and employees often walked to the factory or used the city streetcar line. There was a full station rail stop at the company door.

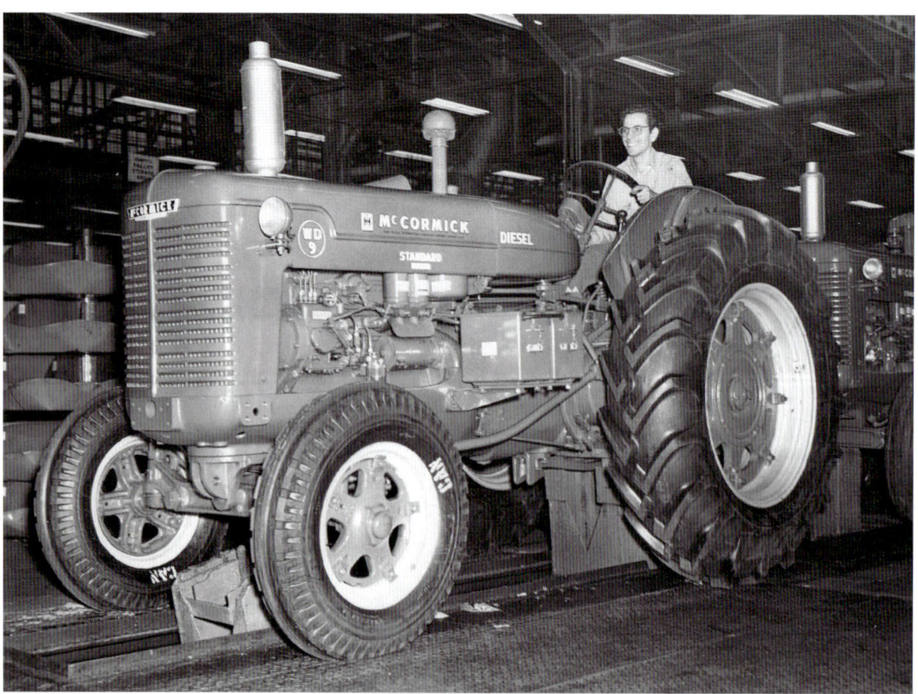

TRACTOR EMPIRE: The International Harvester Corporation was one of the largest farm implement makers in America. It was established in 1847 as the McCormick Reaper Company, a mega Chicago corporation.

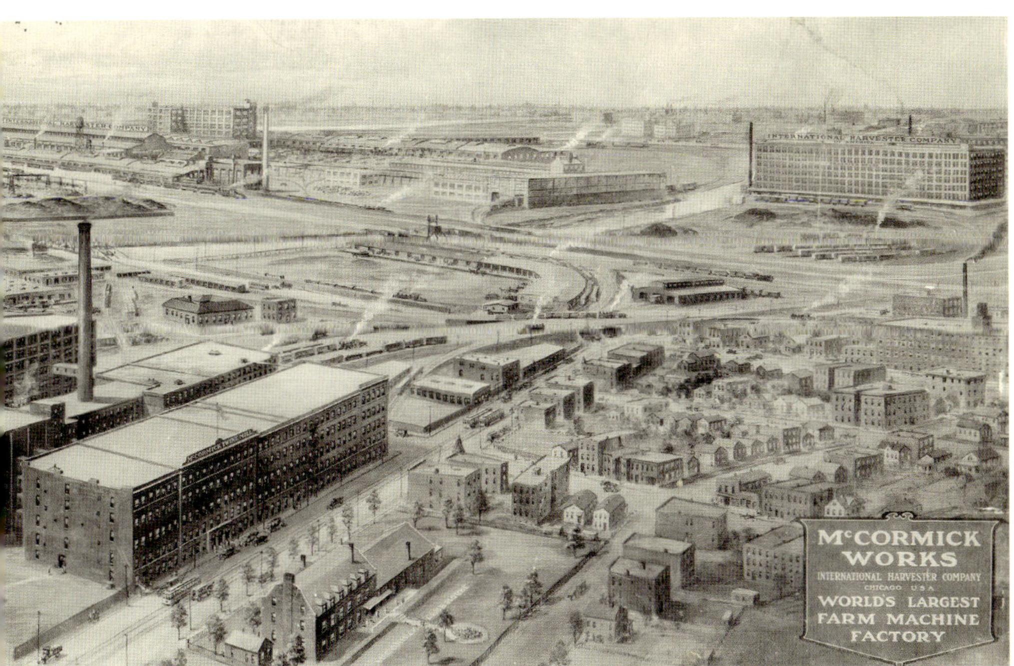

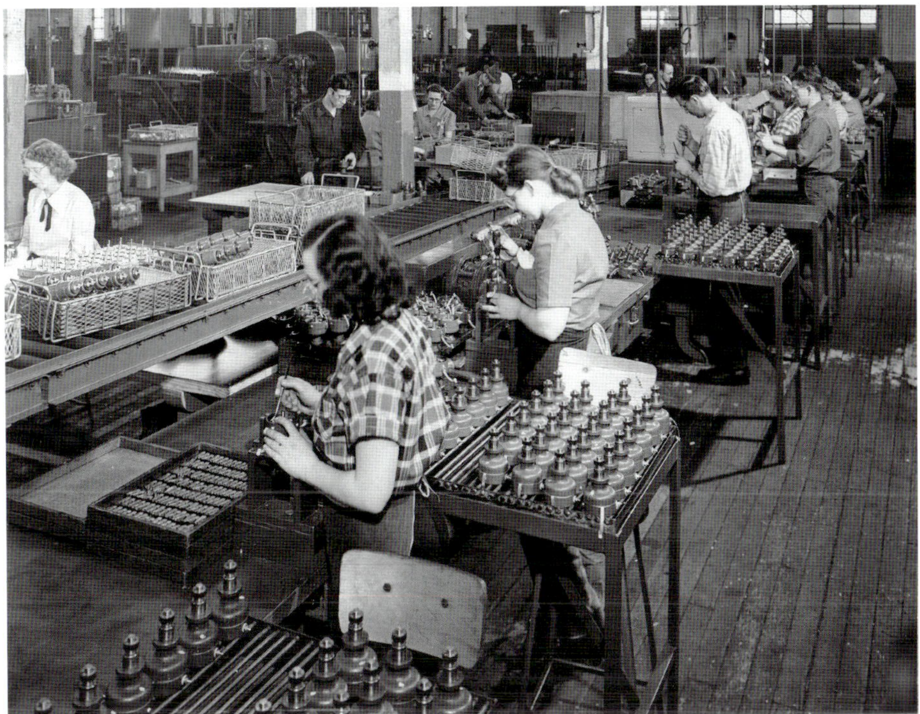

In 1952, the Harvester Company was one of the first major city employers to integrate its workforce. Women and other minorities worked on the assembly line and they were highly productive.

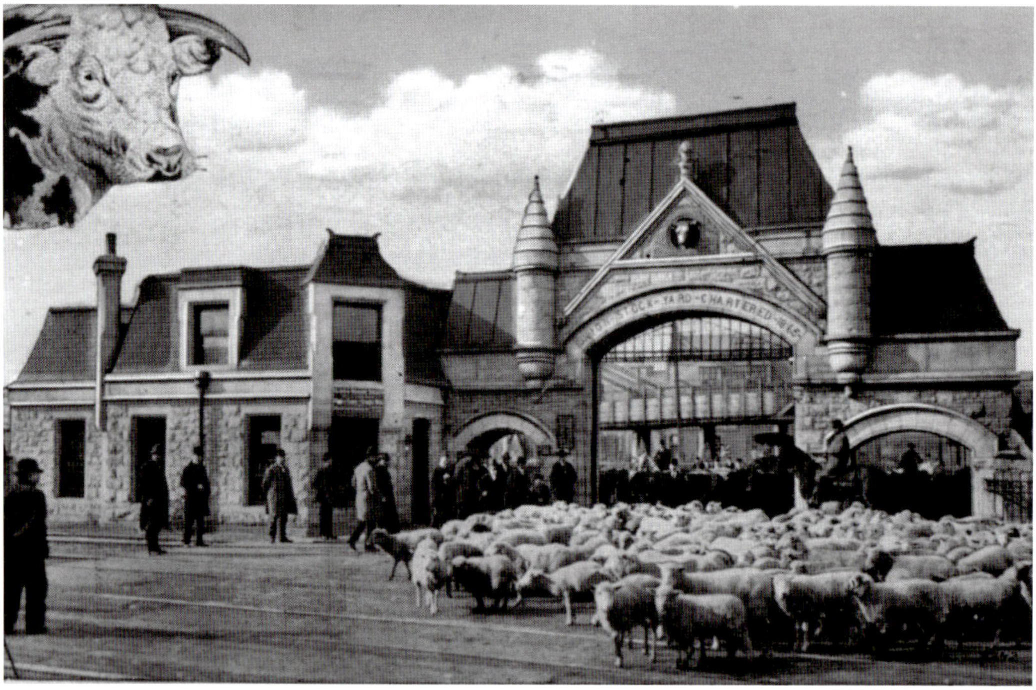

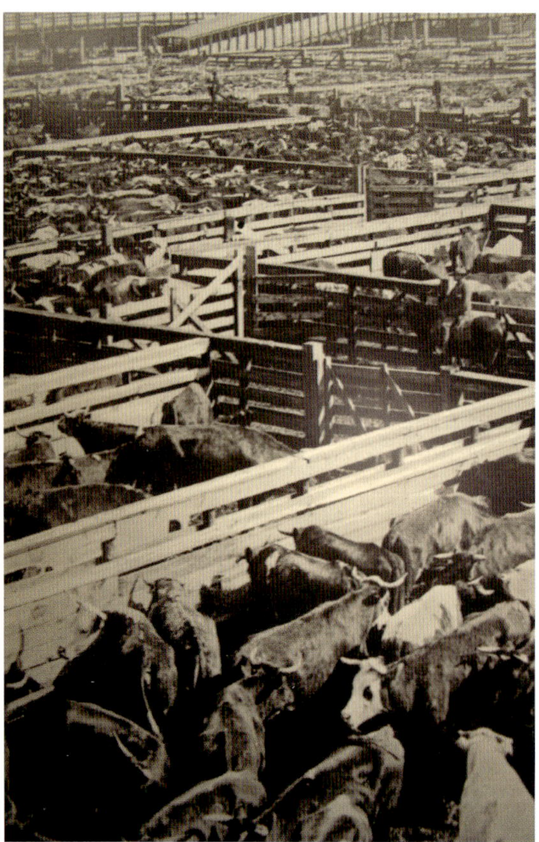

PIG PEN: Based on its central location, Chicago became the stockyard center of America. Farm animals were driven to big processors like Swift and Armour companies. Muckraking journalist, Upton Sinclair, quipped that the meat cutters processed "everything but the squeal."

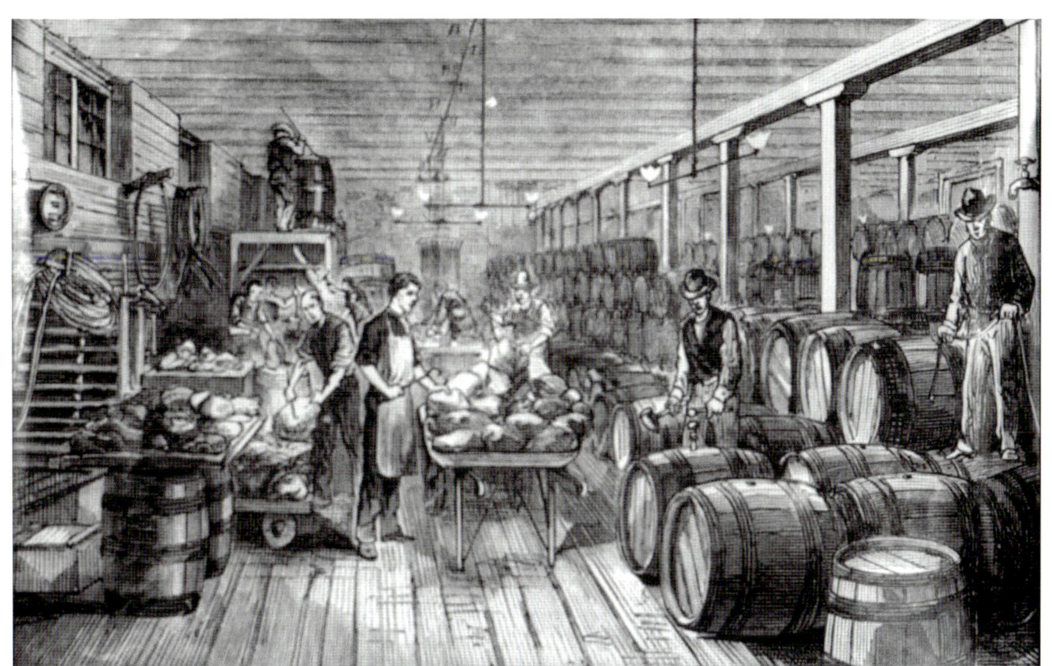

RAIL AND TRUCK: Salting and "pork barreling" meats was the old fashioned way of preservation. Later, refrigerated railroad cars allowed the meat packers to double their productivity. Today, specialty meats are packed and shipped by trucks to grocery stores and restaurants. Chicago's old stockyard area has converted to an industrial park that now houses many new types of clean industry.

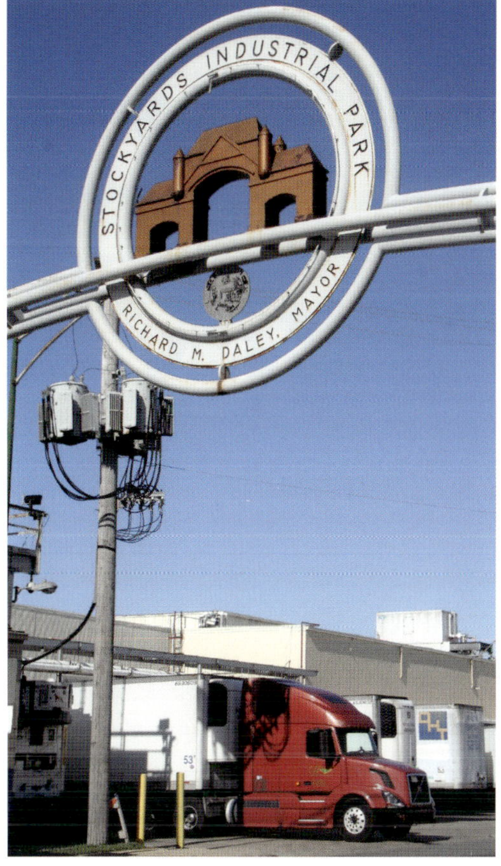

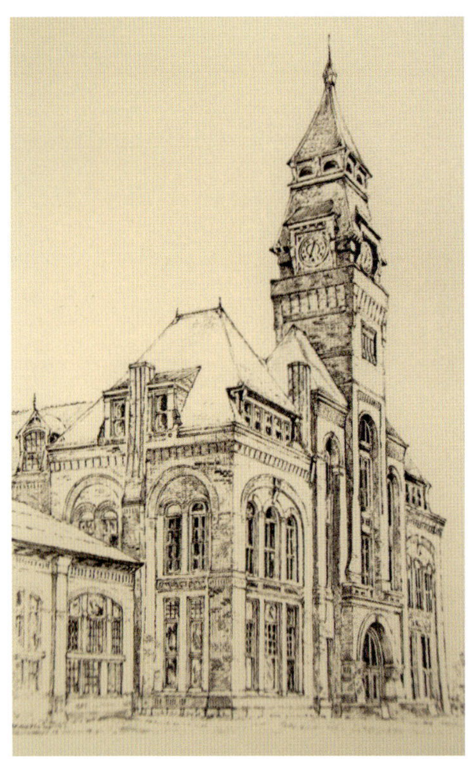

PULLMAN: In 1867, George Pullman created a transit company, brick by brick. The Pullman Palace Car Company made rail travel a luxurious experience. They also made subway cars for the City of Chicago.

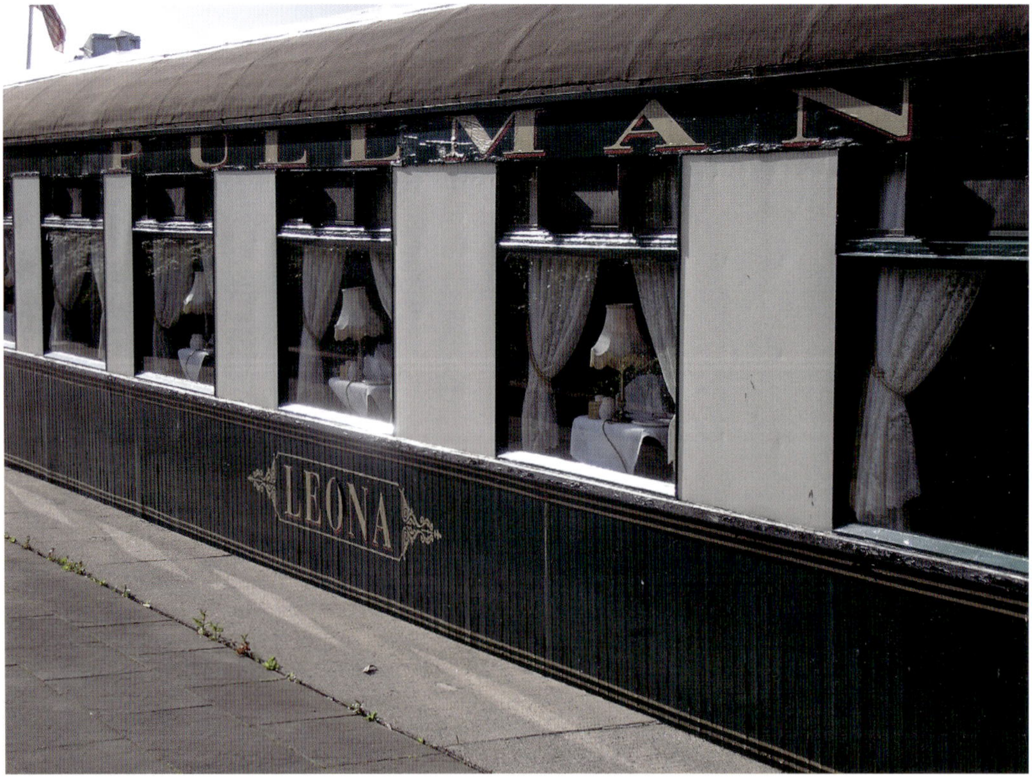

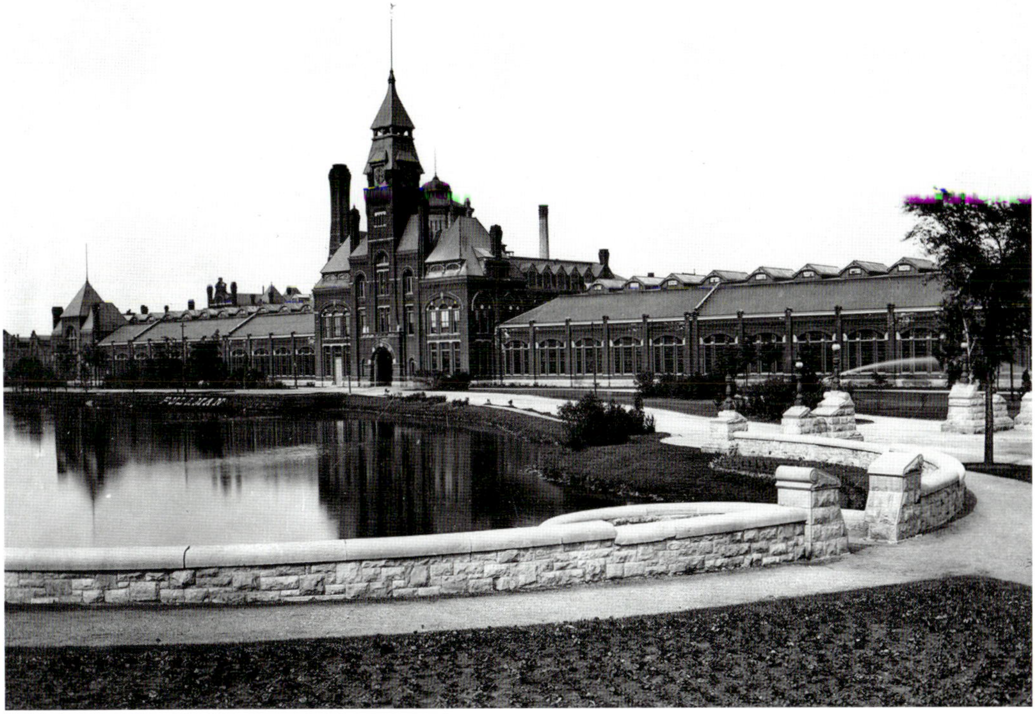

ARCHI-DREAMS: George Pullman was a utopian visionary and patriarch. He hired town planners to carefully integrate worker's housing into the industrial landscape. However, a nationwide labor strike in 1894 spoiled Pullman's dream. Factory workers needed fair wages more than new architecture. Today, the Pullman community is in the midst of a revival as Chicago families search for historic and affordable housing.

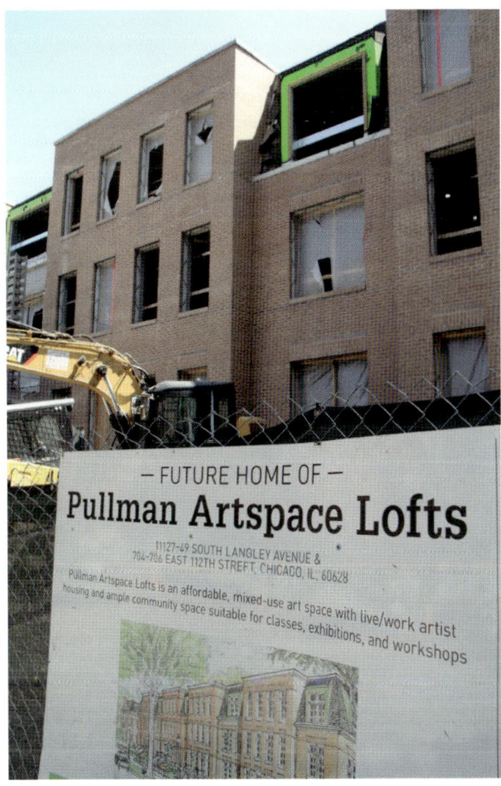

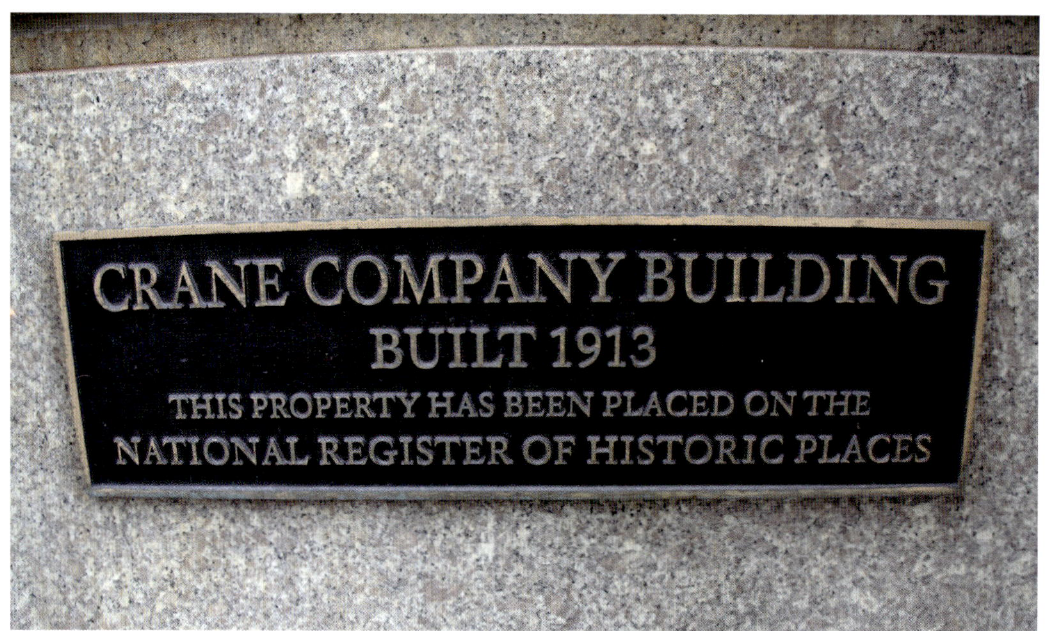

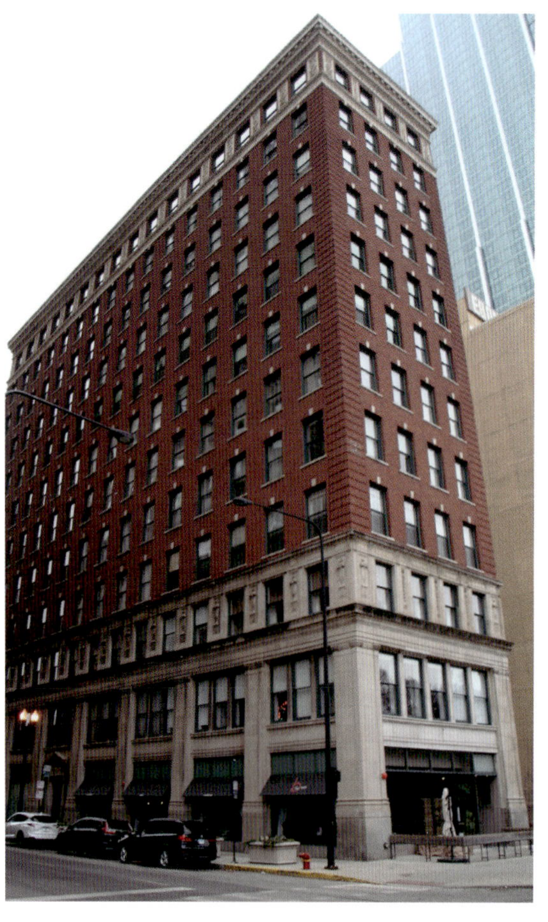

AN EARLY SKYSCRAPER: In 1913, the Crane Company produced iron and brass plumbing fixtures for a growing city. Sinks, tubs, and faucets were required in every new home and business. The foundries were located in forty buildings far from the Loop headquarters. Today, the Crane tower has been converted to condominiums.

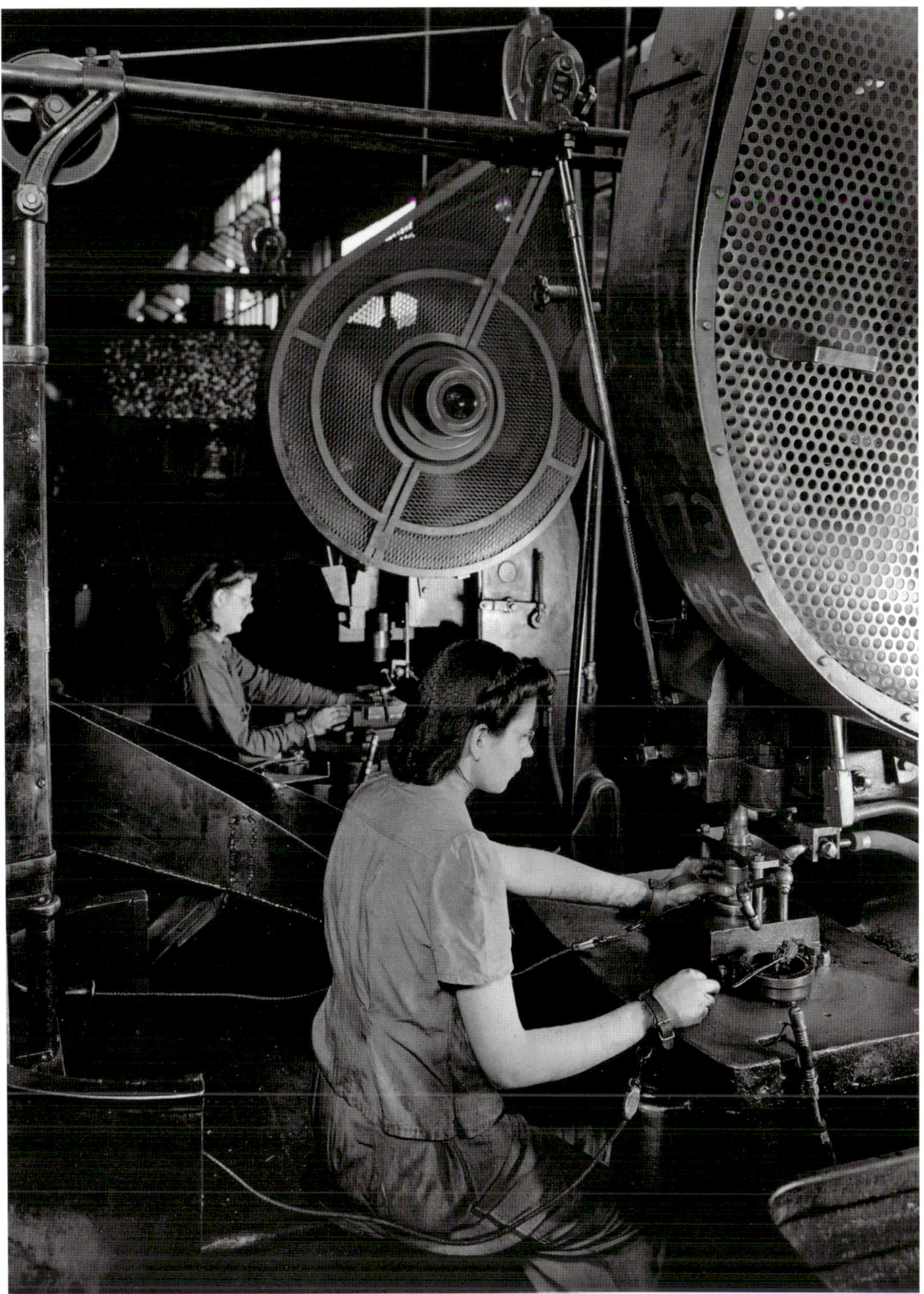

HIGH WIRE ACT: Although Crane offered a reliable wage, the work was dangerous. This woman operated machinery wearing wire restraints. If her hands were pulled into a machine, the trip wires shut down the assembly line immediately.

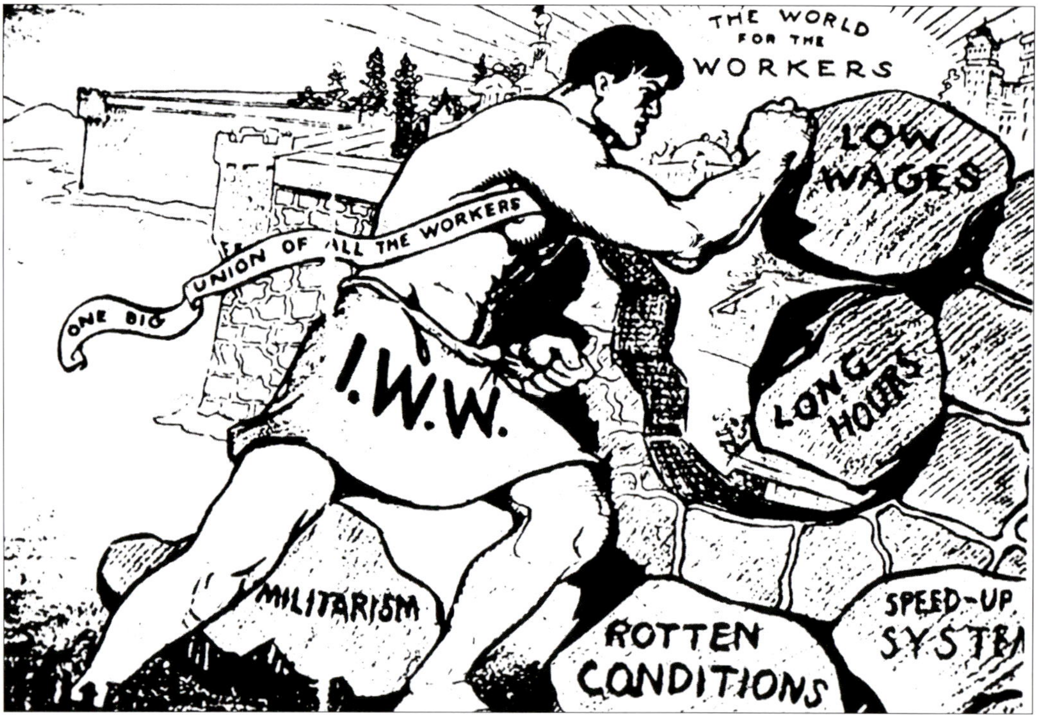

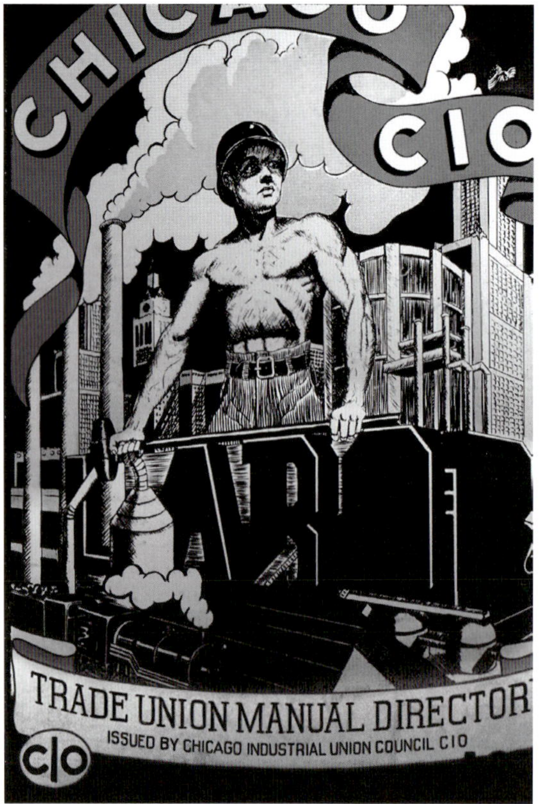

WORKERS FIGHT: The grievances of labor are clearly expressed in this Industrial Workers of the World poster. Not only did they protest working conditions, the I.W.W. campaigned against labor's participation in World War I. By 1937, the Congress of Industrial Organization (C.I.O.) took a giant step beyond the I.W.W. in getting full recognition for coal miners, automotive workers, and most laborers in heavy industry to receive wages on a union scale.

2

Manufacturing

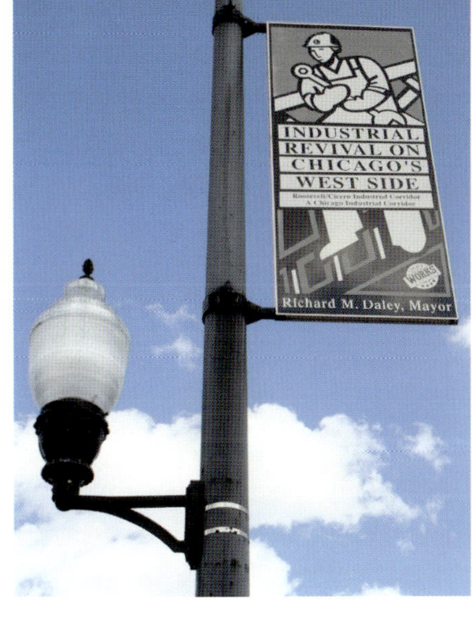

From approximately 1875 to 1975, Chicago excelled in manufacturing. (The rise and fall of Chicago's productivity is a story told in greater detail in the introductory portion of this book.) Chicago manufacturers created an array of popular products: men's clothing, typewriters, beer, elevators, candy, bicycles, musical instruments, telephones, bowling balls, and diesel engines are some examples. The companies that produced these products earned millions of dollars and employed many thousands of blue-collar and white-collar workers. Several manufacturers in this book operated small "industrial villages" that have been the subjects of several sociological studies on Chicago.

Of the ten manufacturing giants featured in this chapter, only four continue their product line as name- brands today. The other six firms have been sold as new brands, merged, and moved out of town, or closed forever. Still consumers around the world will not forget original brands like Sunbeam, Radio Flyer, Bell & Howell, Dr. Scholl and more. Today, manufacturers that are prosperous survivors in Chicagoland are Motorola, Kraft, Weber Grill, and other major brands, already more than a half-century old.

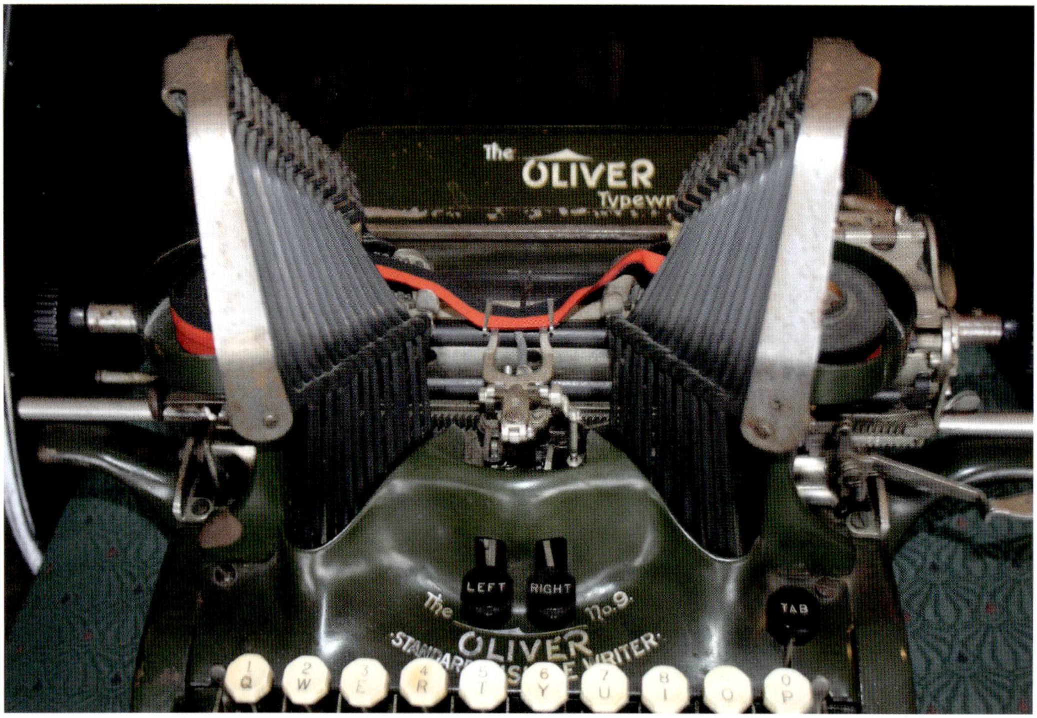

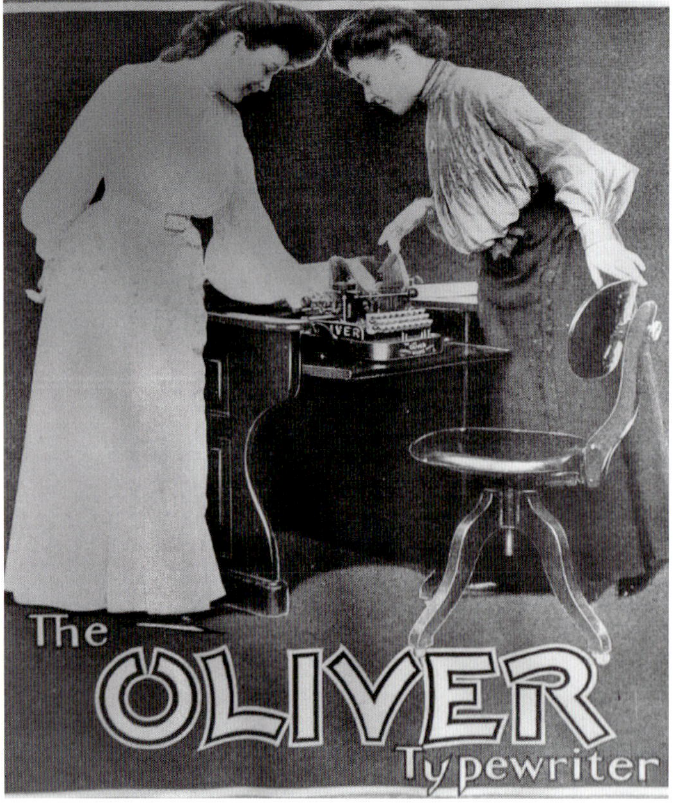

Office Machines:

The typewriter was crucial to the revolution in American business machines at the turn of the twentieth century. In 1907, the Oliver Company brought typing technology to Chicago. It standardized business correspondence, which brought the company many customers and high income.

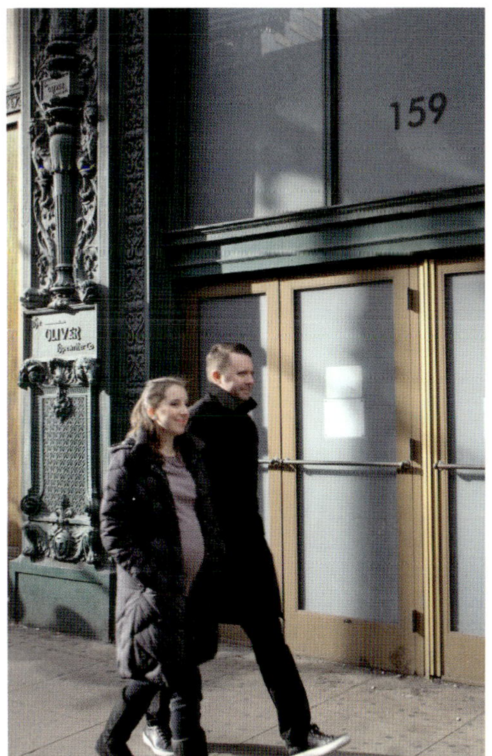

IN THE LOOP: Building a business on Dearborn Street in Chicago required large capital. This cast iron facade of Oliver is an architectural landmark. Today, the old Oliver building has new tenants in the heart of the city's redesigned theater district.

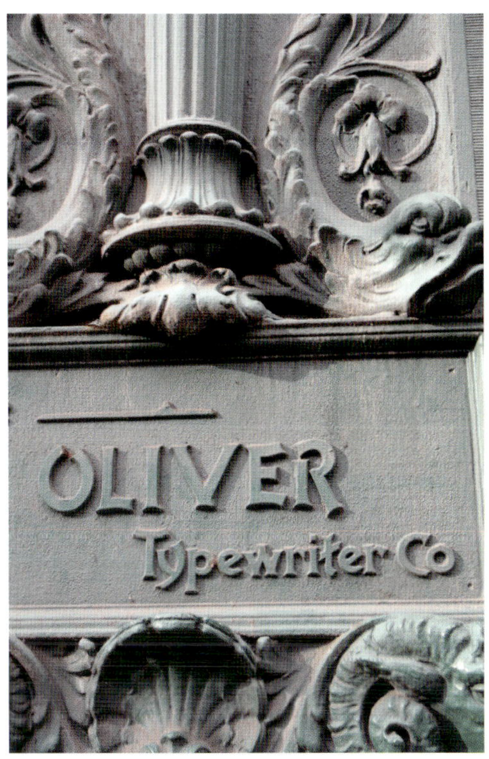

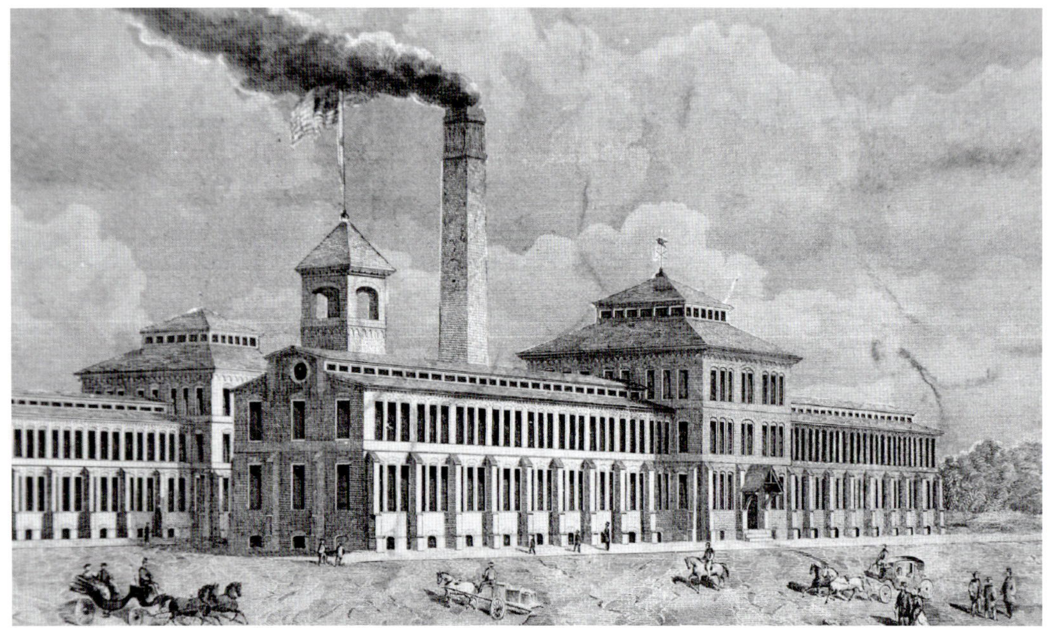

ELGIN RISES: Before the U.S. Civil War, the Elgin Watch Company produced timepieces for a young America living in an age of horse and wagon. The company hired skilled men and women for delicate piecework. The Elgin operation could be viewed as primitive technology in an era of heavy industry.

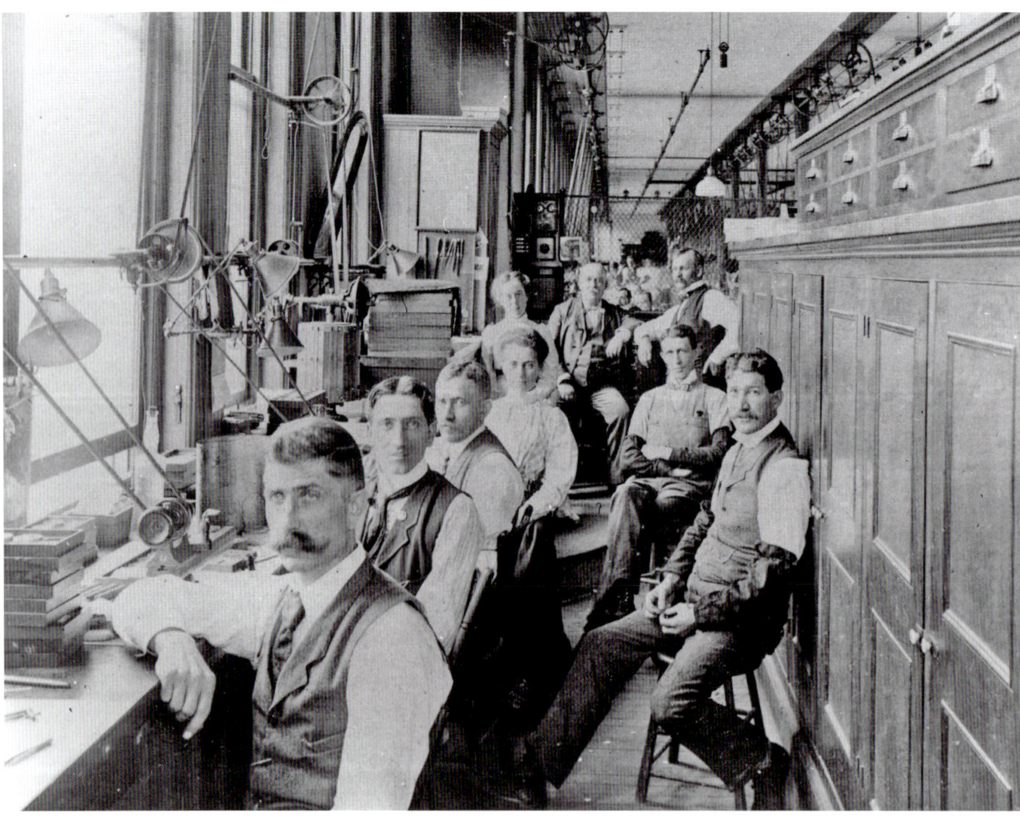

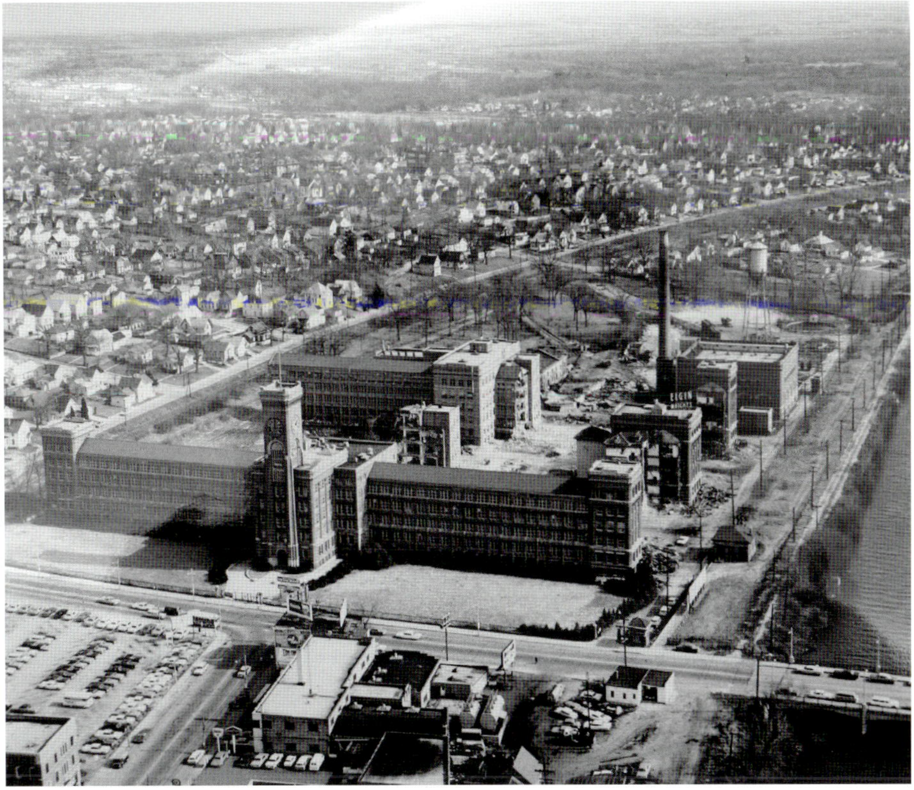

ELGIN FALLS: Elgin Watch became a national brand by the twentieth century, and about half the watches sold in America were Elgin's. The factory expanded over decades to take up many city blocks. However, by the 1960s, overseas competition caused Elgin to falter. By 1965, the factory was demolished.

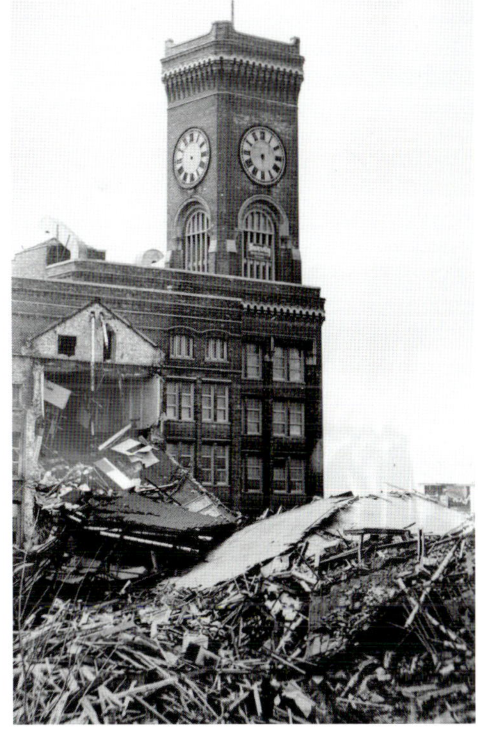

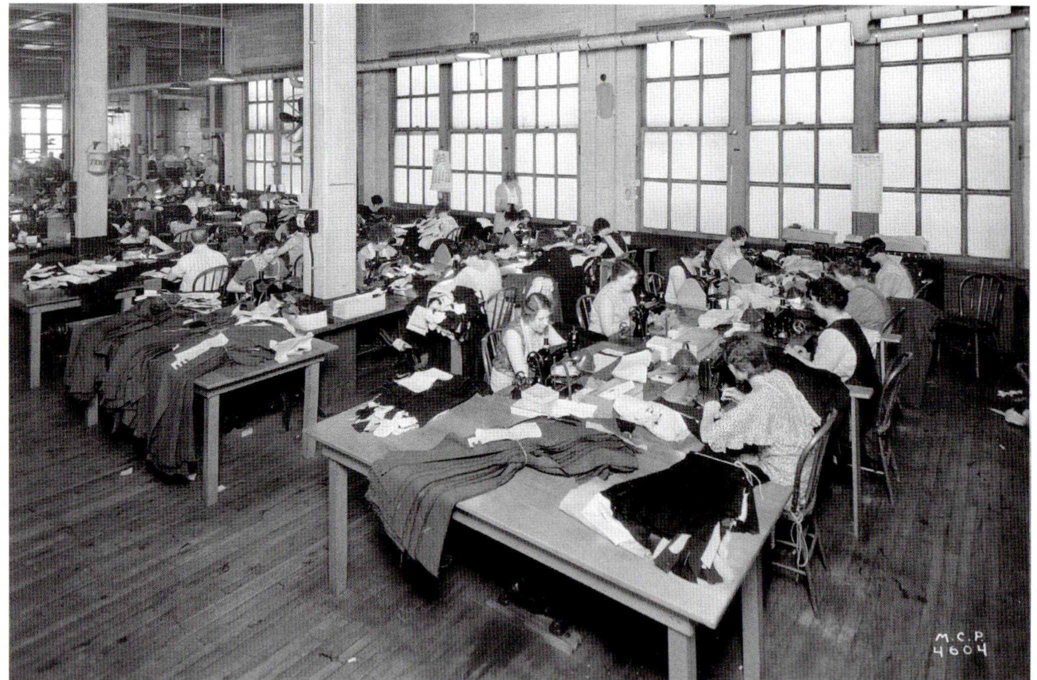

SUITING UP: Hart Schaffner & Marx has been a popular clothing maker for more than 100 years. Located on Chicago's Near Westside, thousands of immigrant Jewish, Italian, and Mexican tailors found work at the factory. Hart Schaffner & Marx's men's suits were trendsetting and fashionable. The company partnered with Pierre Cardin and Christian Dior on many styling projects.

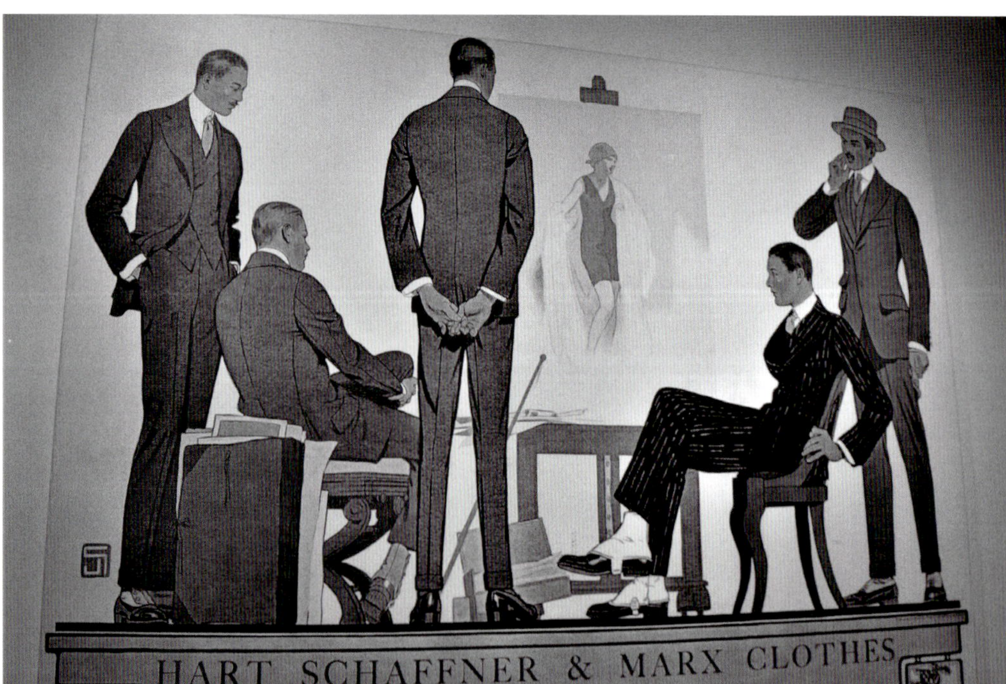

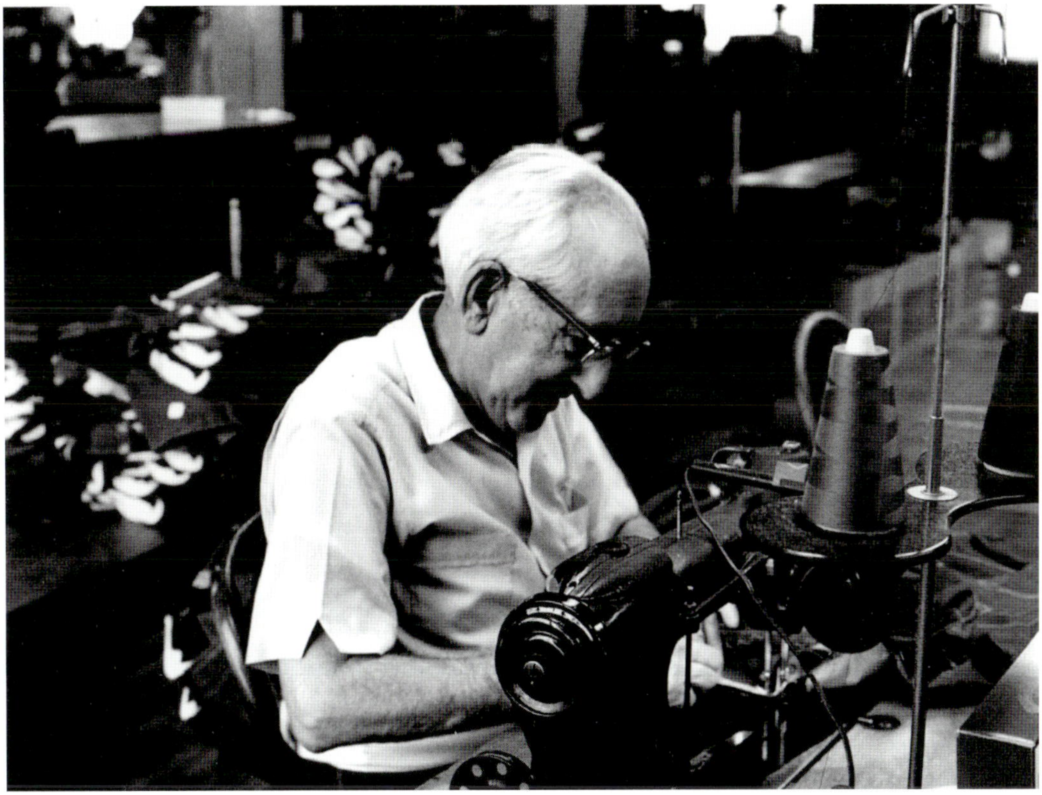

Today's Trends: Eventually the company changed their name to Hart-Marx and moved to the Chicago suburb of Des Plaines. Skilled tailors make a variety of clothing items. During the Covid crisis, the company even designed face masks. The old Westside factory, built in 1915, has been converted to a condominium project called Haberdasher Square.

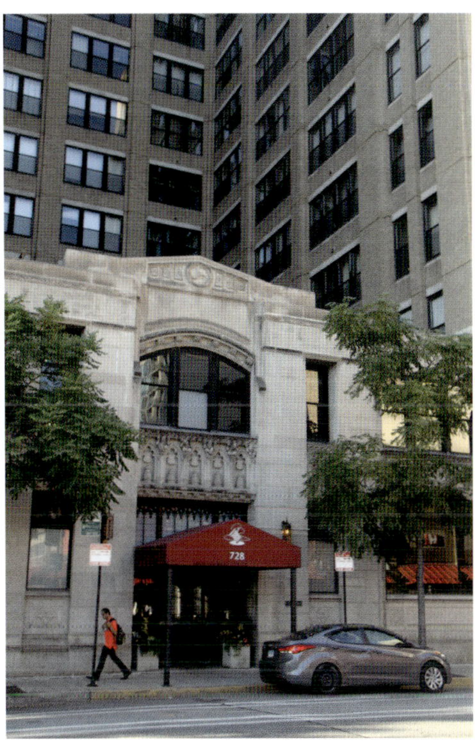

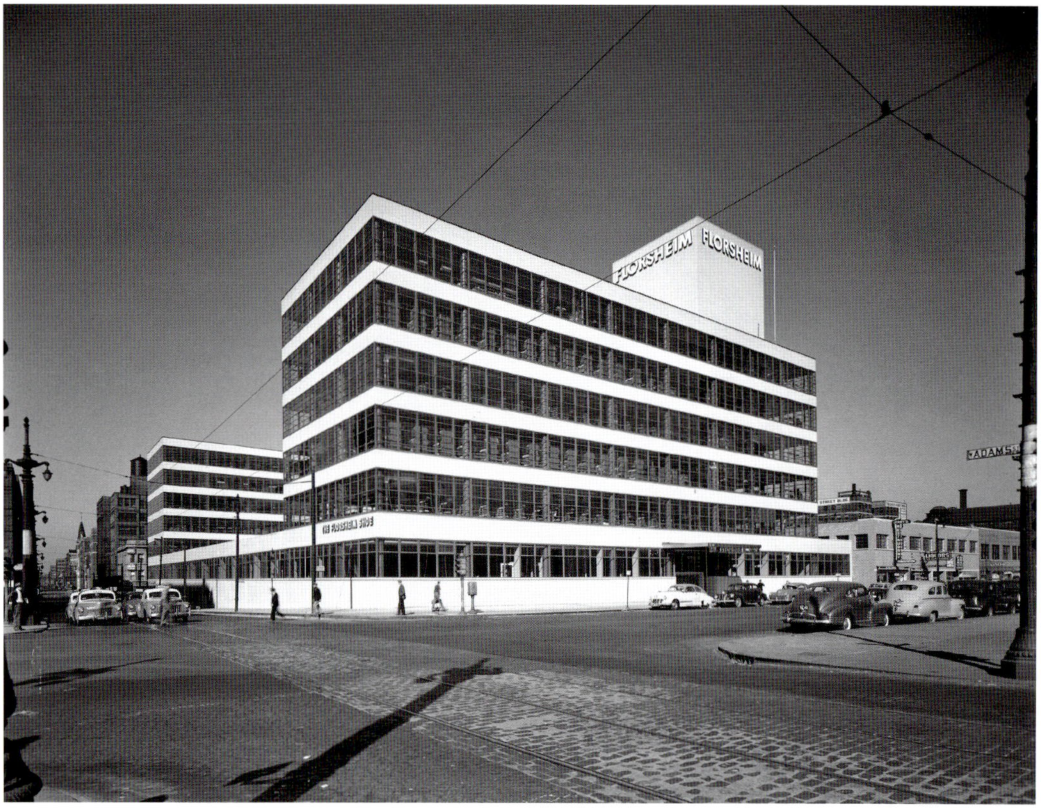

A Sleek Prototype: The Florsheim Shoe Company building was designed in 1926 with aerodynamic lines that presaged the Art Deco architecture of the 1930s. Today, minimalist styled office spaces in Chicago echo the design of the Florsheim factory. Windows were spacious and allowed plenty of sunlight and fresh air for the men and women who worked there.

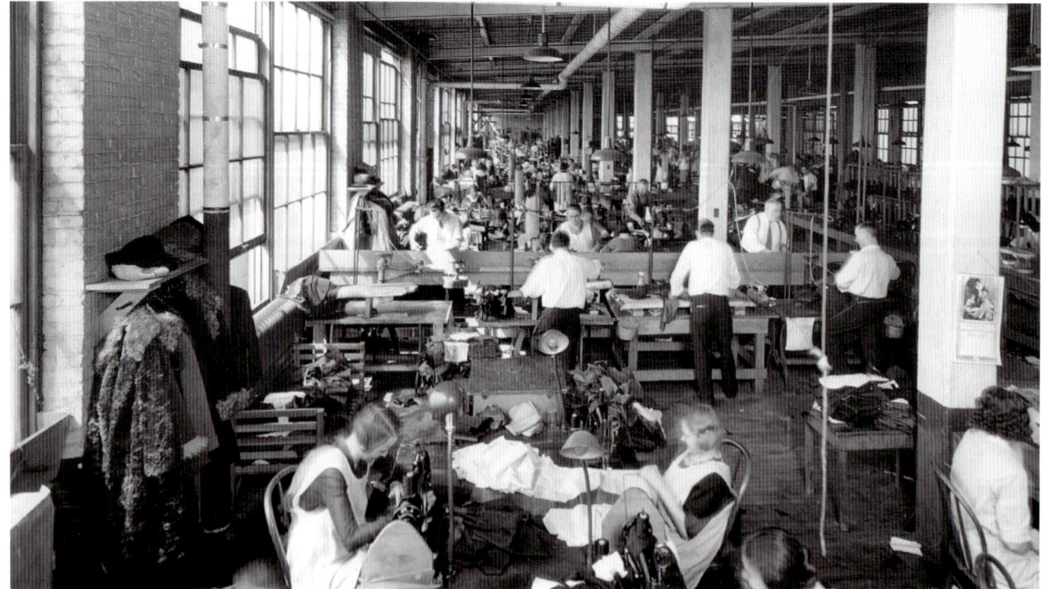

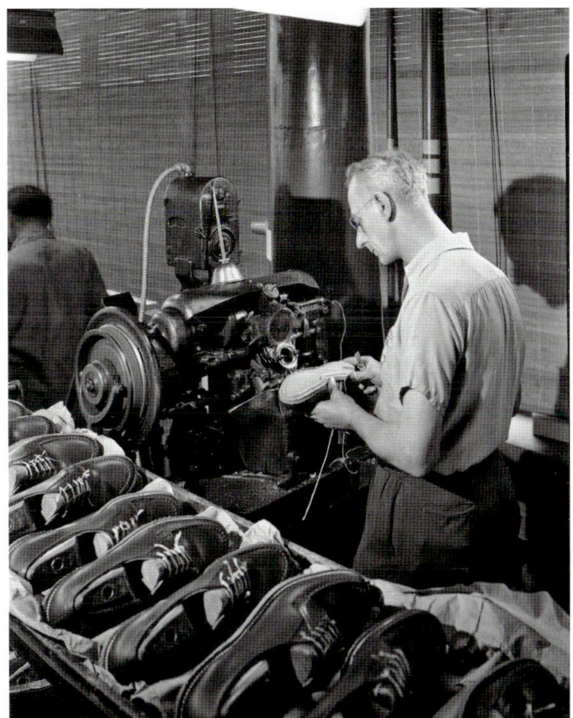

Skeletal Architecture:
This Florsheim assembly line shows workers stitching shoe soles. These work-shoes were forerunners of the Dockers casual shoe style for men. Today, the Florsheim factory has become a fashionable condominium location. Chicago architect, Alfred Alschuler, stylized the original 1892 factory and made it a landmark building.

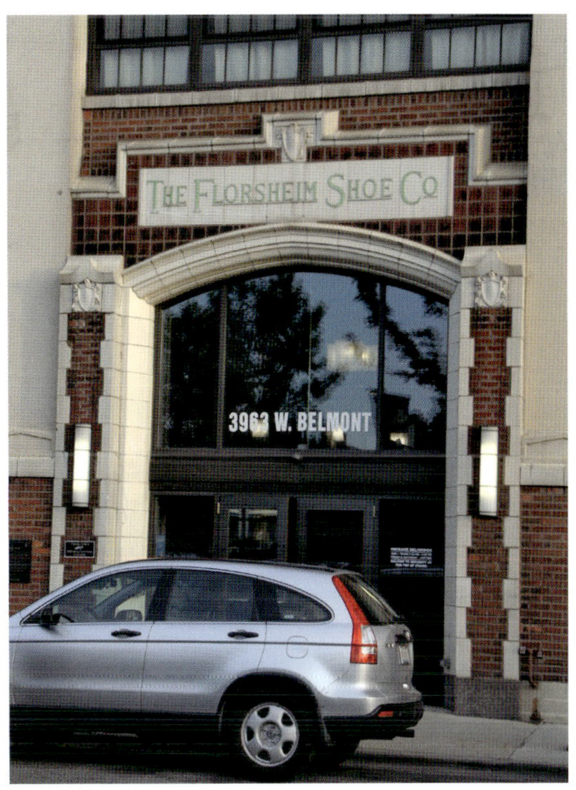

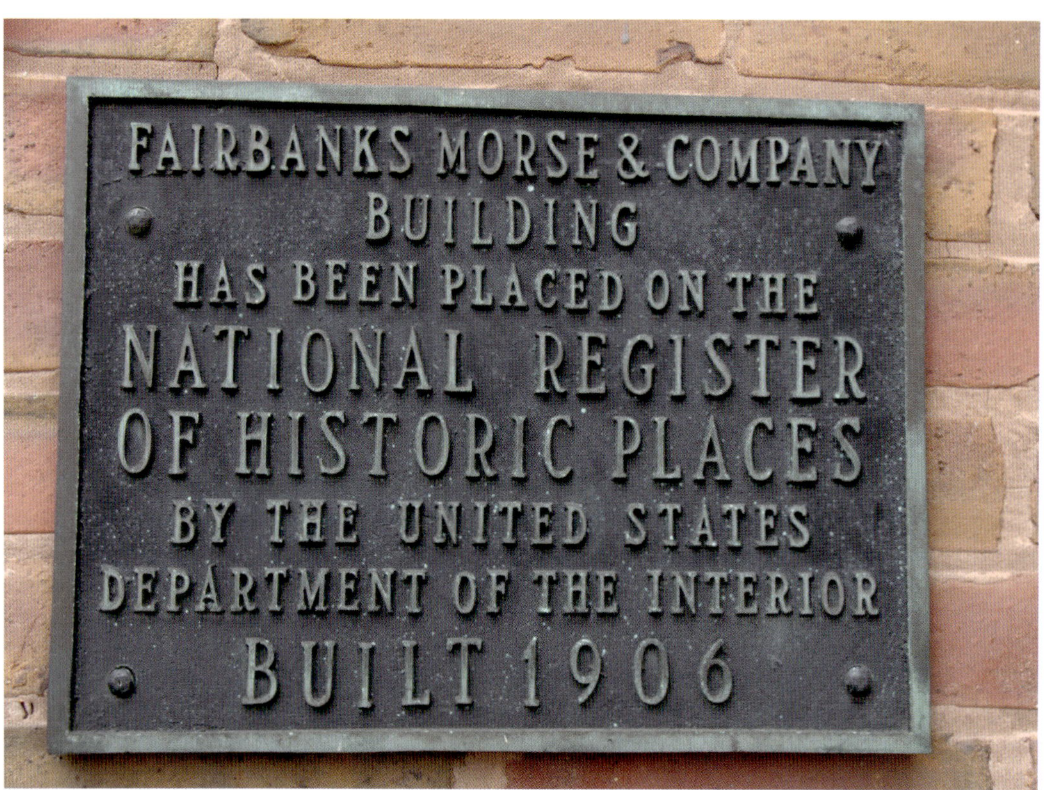

ENGINE OF PROSPERITY: The Fairbanks-Morse Company began as a windmill factory in Chicago, but converted to making mega diesel engines (12 cylinders) by 1915. As one of Chicago's first multi-national companies, Fairbanks-Morse developed branches in Latin America and Australia.

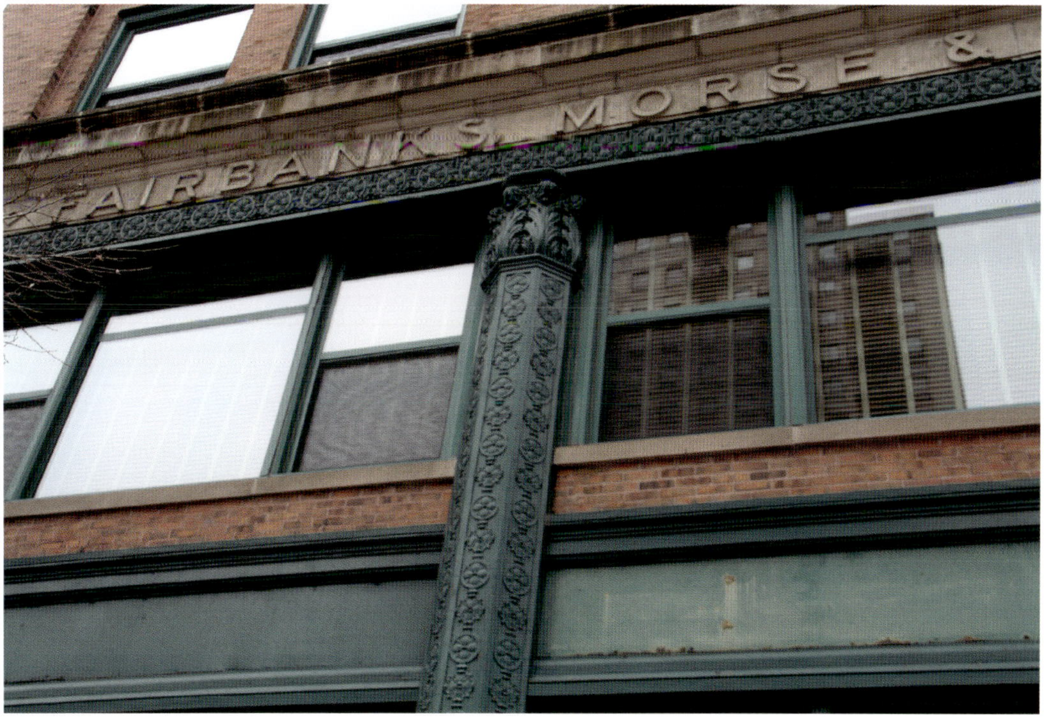

HIGH STATUS: Fairbanks-Morse wanted a stylish Prairic School design for its headquarters. The building achieved city landmark status, and today it is a popular loft-styled condominium at a trendy address in Chicago's South Loop downtown district.

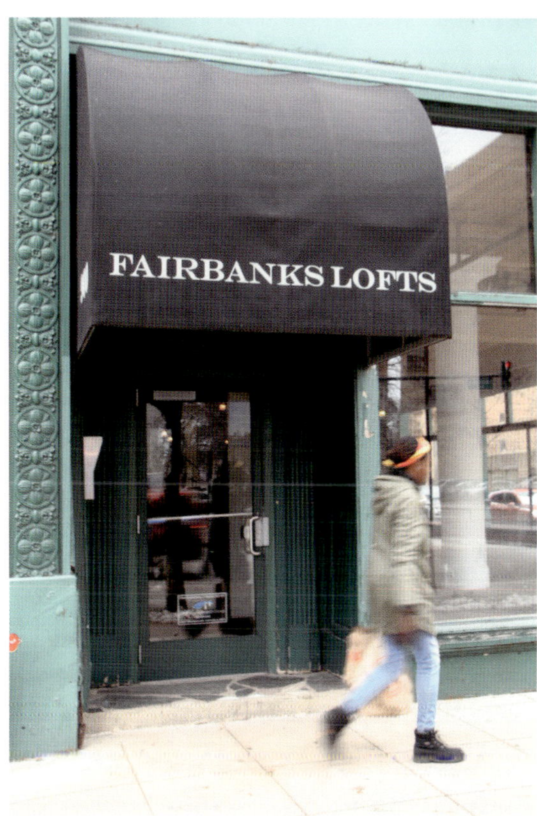

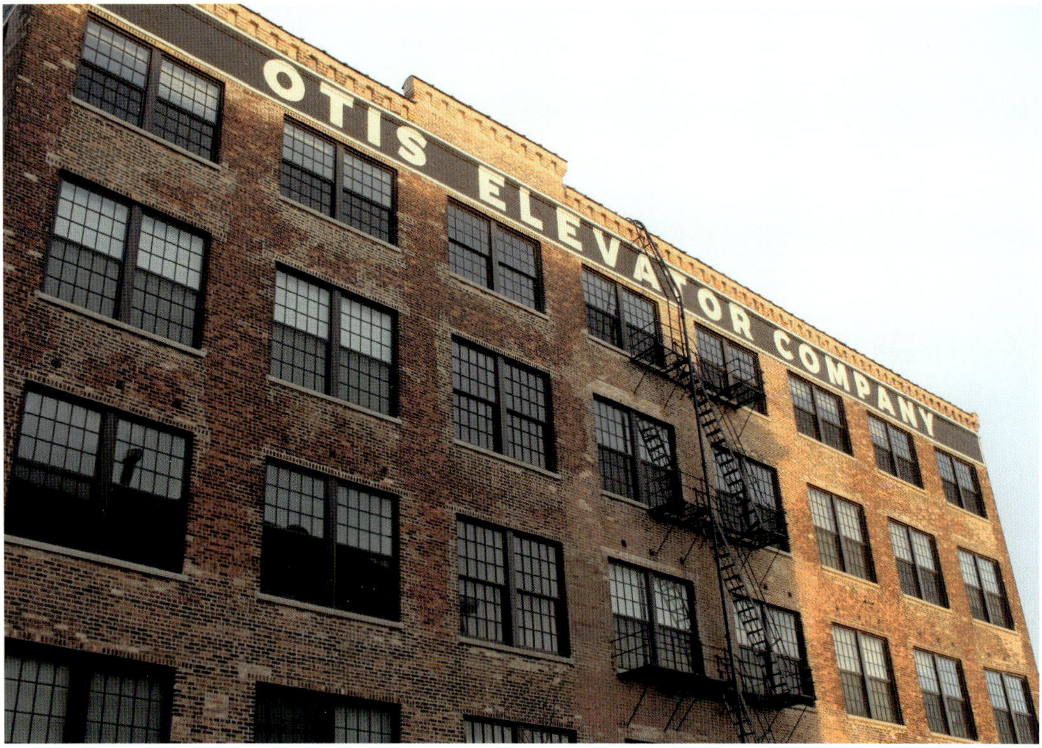

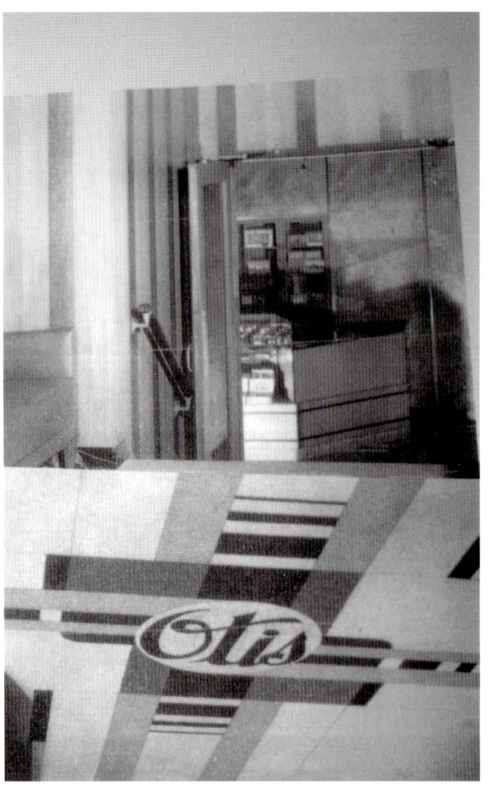

LOFTY HEIGHTS: Though not invented in Chicago, the Otis Elevator Company arrived in the Pilsen neighborhood as early as 1914. Chicago, known for its skyscrapers, created plenty of clients for Otis services. This elaborate Art Deco styled lobby comes from an Otis office, hand decorated with Italian terrazzo flooring.

DIVERSITY: Established in 1848, Brunswick is currently the oldest public corporation in Chicago. From vulcanized rubber and plastic, Brunswick produces bowling balls, car tires, billiard balls, 45rpm records, and boat hulls. It is truly a diversified corporation today. Today, Columbia College occupies the original factory building on South Wabash Street while Brunswick occupies a modern corporate tower downtown.

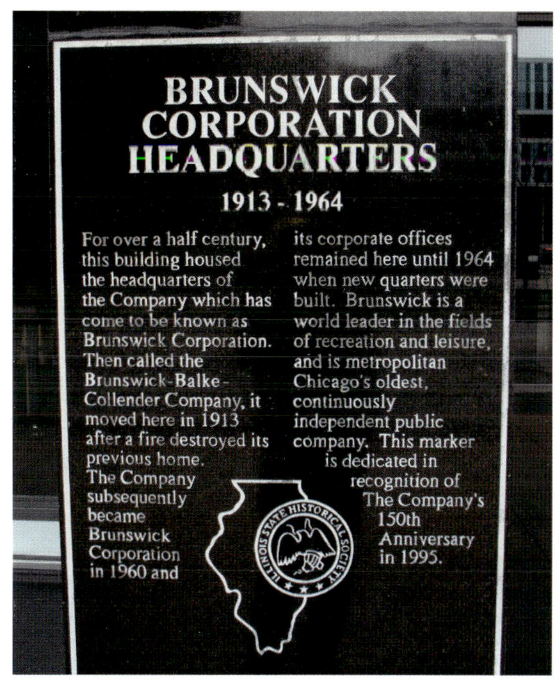

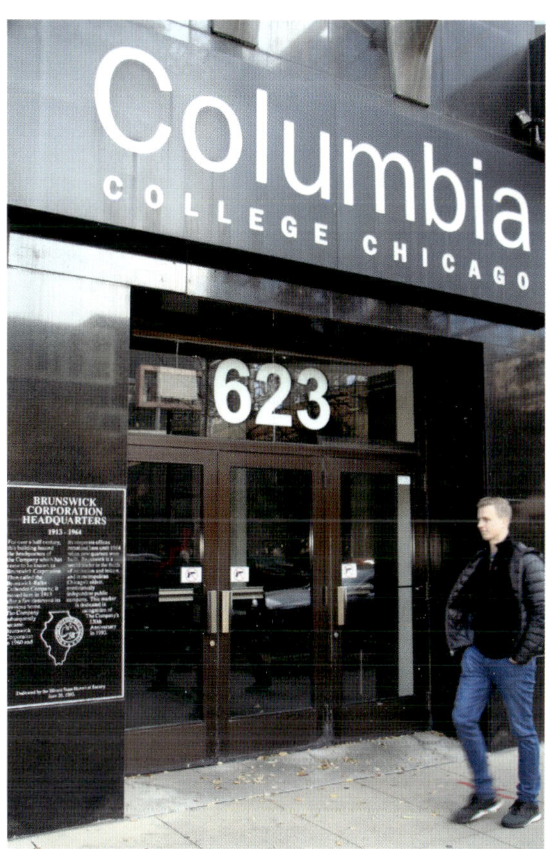

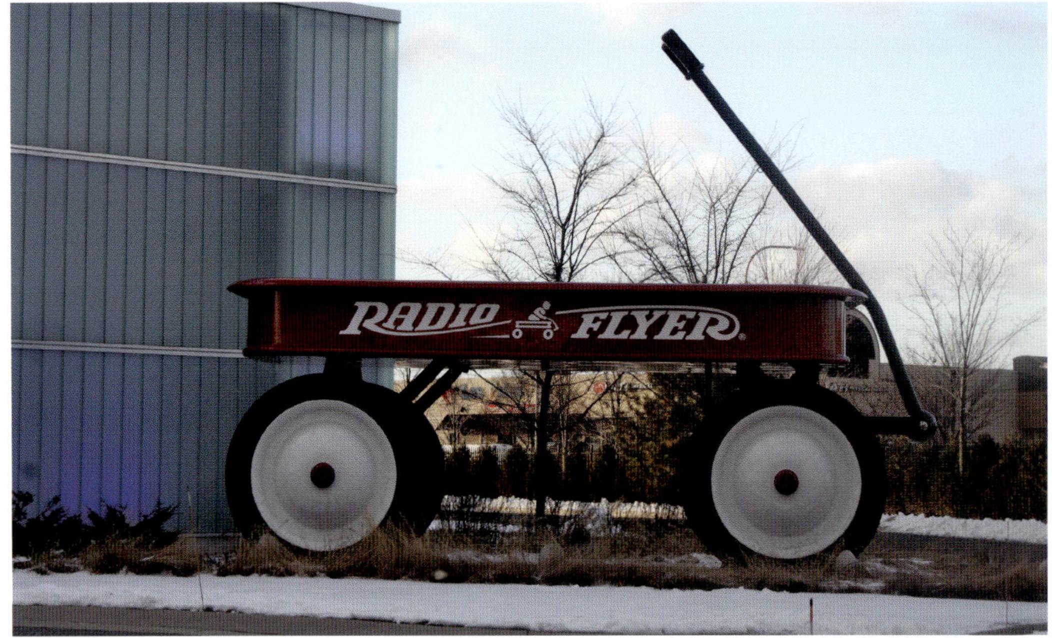

ON THE RADIO: In 1927, Radio flyer took the classic toy, a wooden wagon, and converted it to sturdy metal. The first models sold for less than $5. To commemorate this achievement, the company displays this giant wagon on the lawn of its headquarters in Chicago. The company carefully preserves its history, like this boardroom photo taken in the 1940s.

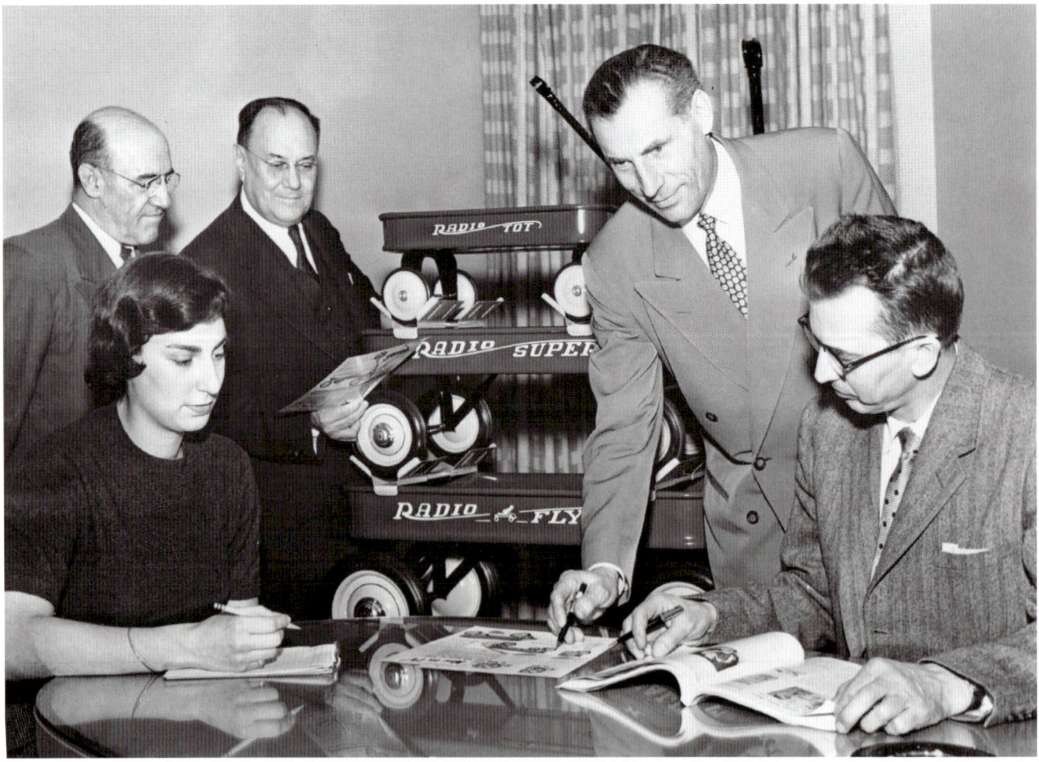

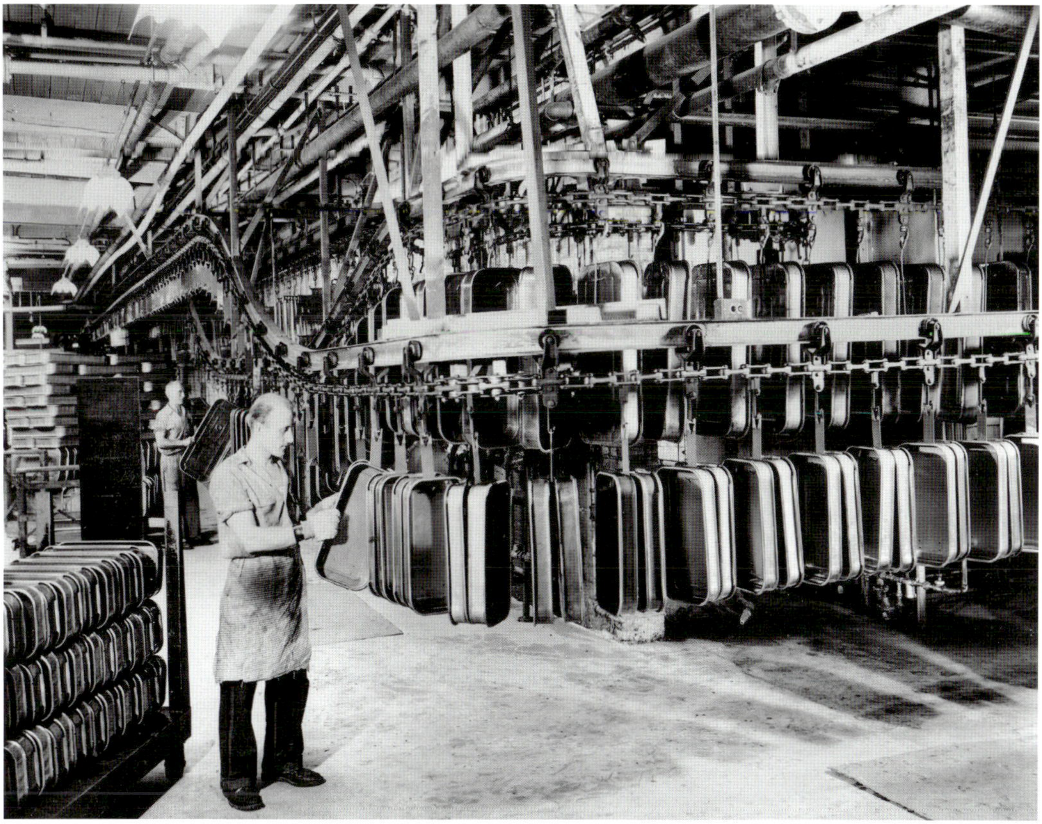

ASSEMBLY LINES: In this factory, Radio Flyer metal stamps its deluxe wagons, complete with headlights and hubcaps. Recently the company designed a "TESLA model" that children can drive at 6 mph. This banner on Grand Avenue in Chicago marks 100 years of toy wagon production.

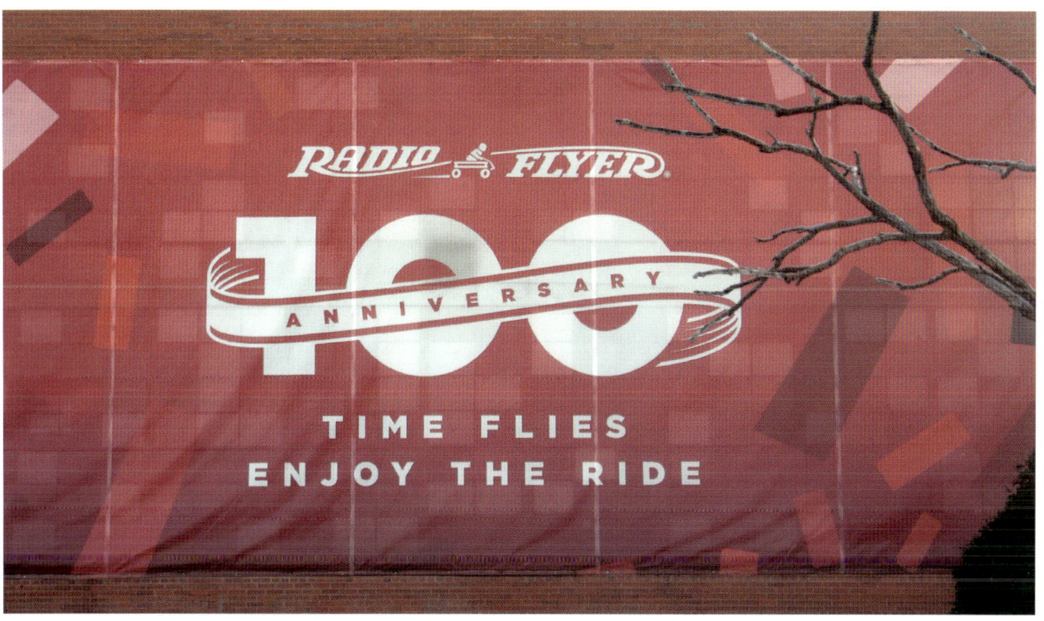

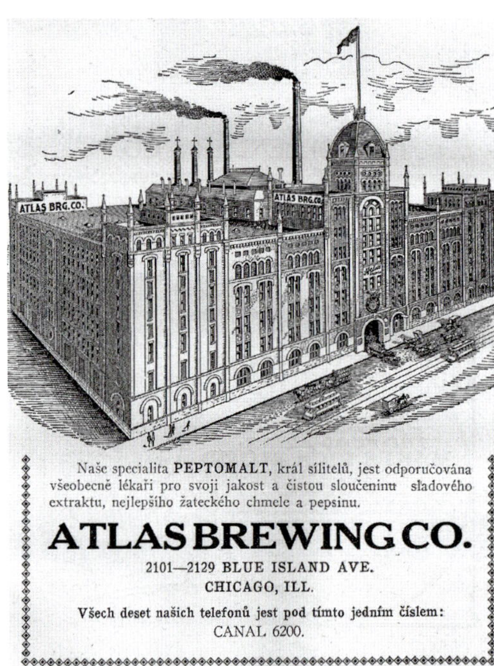

BEER MANUFACTURING: Many European immigrants brought brewing skills to Chicago. The Atlas Company made a popular brew in the Pilsen neighborhood using a heavy dose of malt in the mix. The Schoenhoffen Brewery was established in 1860 by a Jewish beer baron who decorated the front of the factory with a bust of himself, in toga. In more recent times, the bust was stolen by robbers who broke through the third-floor brick wall from the inside!

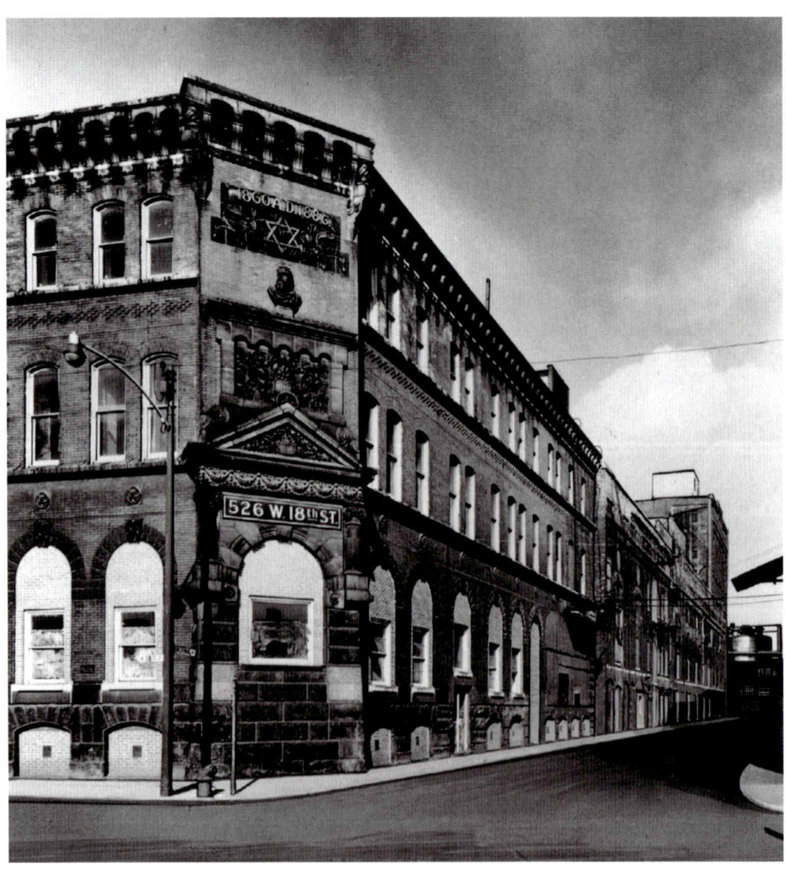

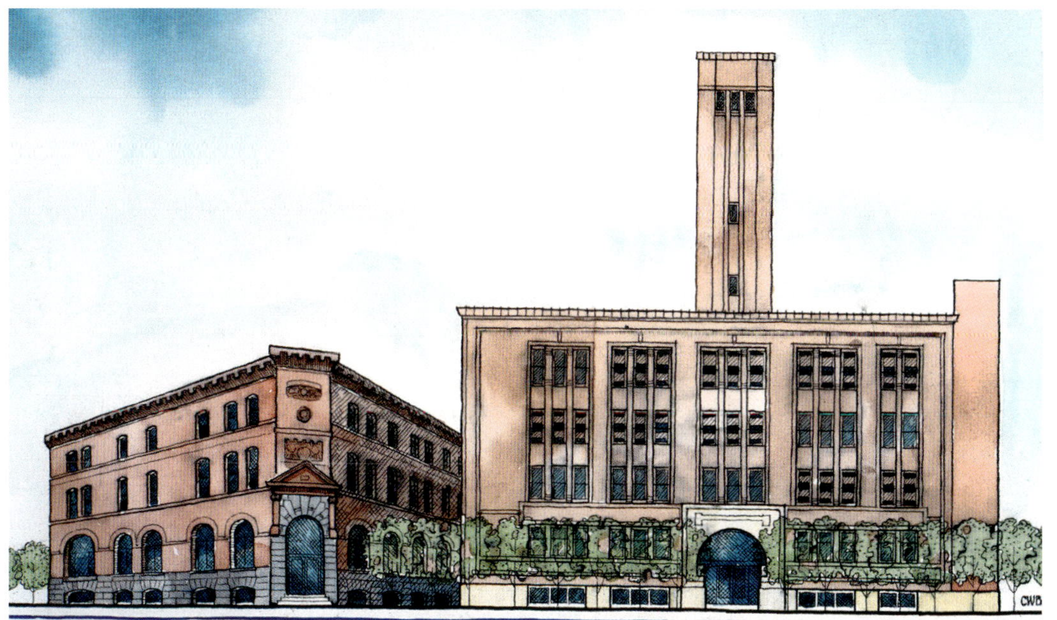

MODERN BREWING: Today the Schoenhoffen factory has been repurposed as apartment spaces and offices. This architectural drawing features the red brick nineteenth-century building with a twenty-first century interior. A new trend among beer makers today is micro-brewing. The Goose Island Brewery is one of the first micro-operations in Chicago. Once a fledgling small business, the Goose Label is well known and profitable throughout the Midwest today.

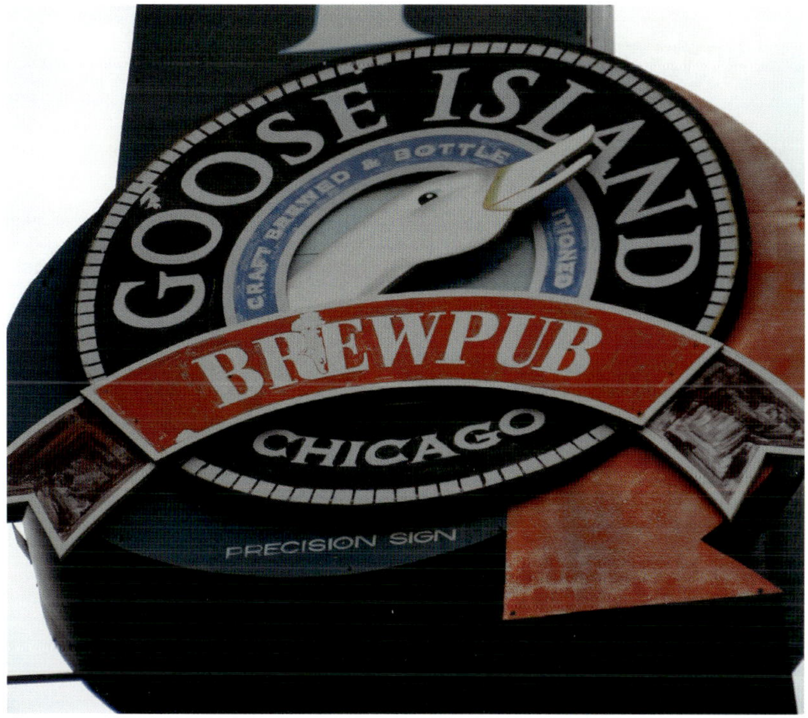

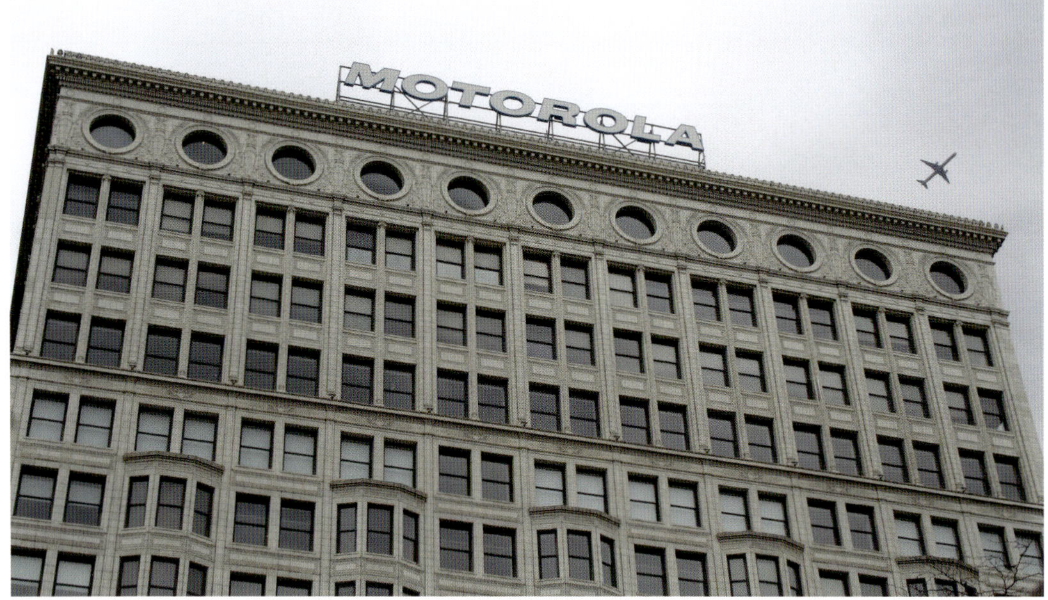

MAJOR LEAGUE: The Motorola Corporation is a long-term survivor in the history of American electronics. Pictured here is the downtown Chicago campus of Motorola housed in a Daniel Burnham designed classic structure, the Railway Exchange Building (1904). The suburban tower of Motorola houses the research and development activity that is cutting edge for the company.

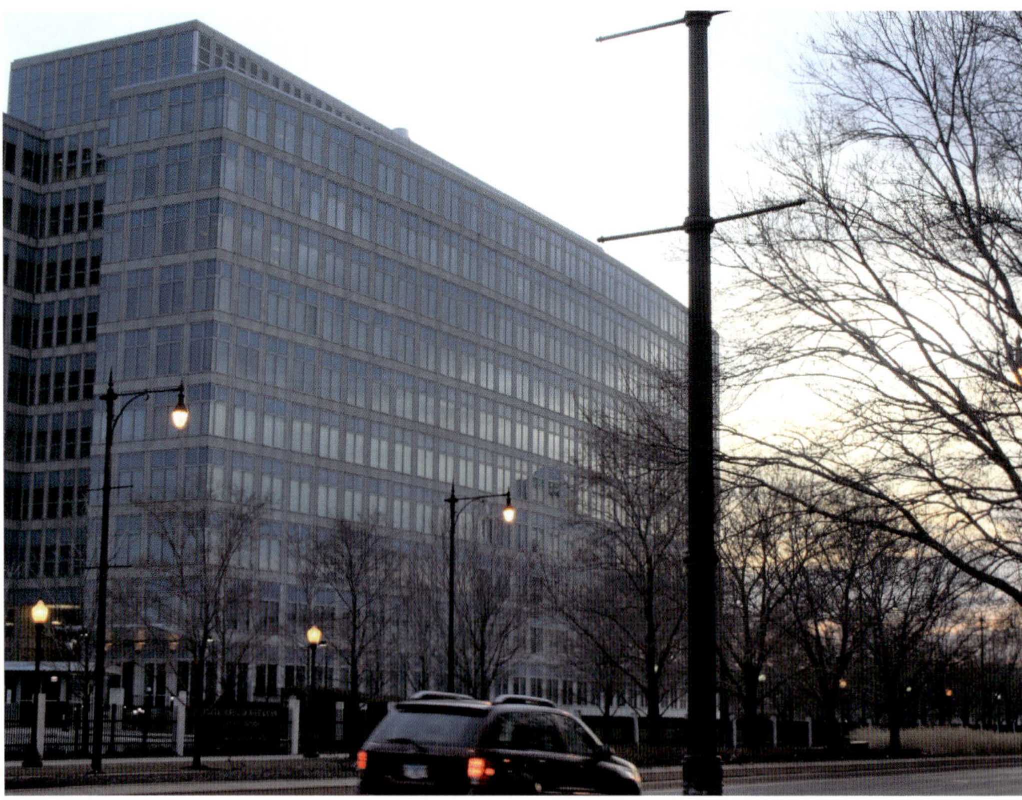

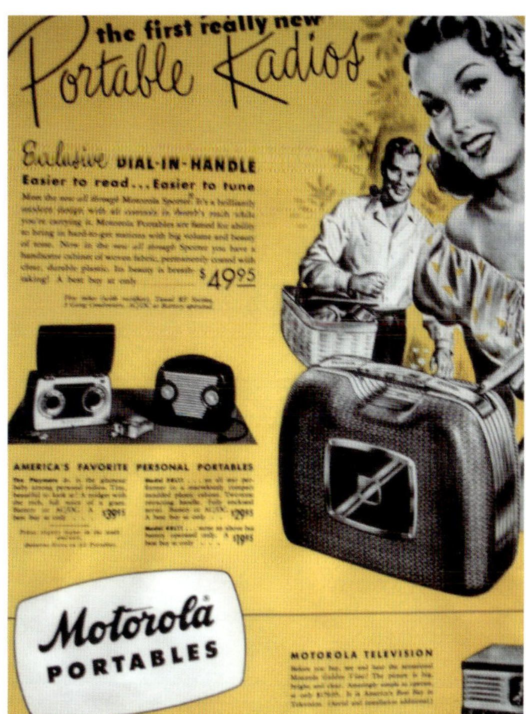

FROM DESKTOPS TO HANDSETS:
When Motorola was first launched, it produced portable radios and walkie-talkie devices. Today, Motorola is involved in many facets of high technology. The Razor brand cell phones of the 1990s were a highly profitable product.

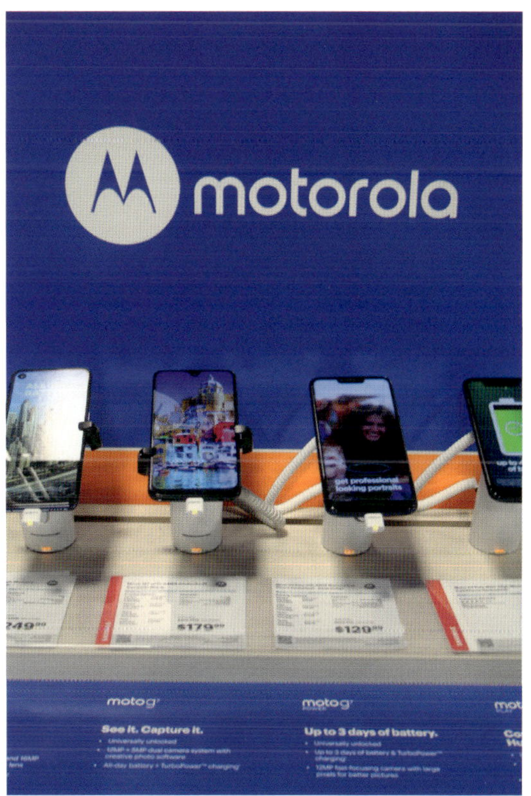

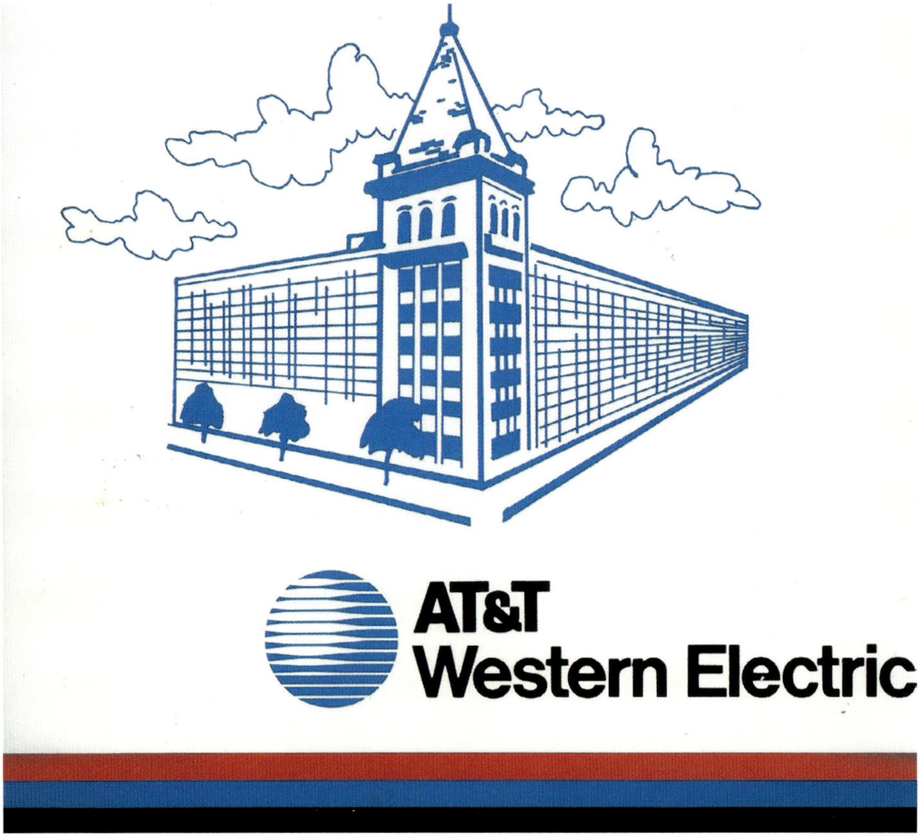

AT&T
Western Electric

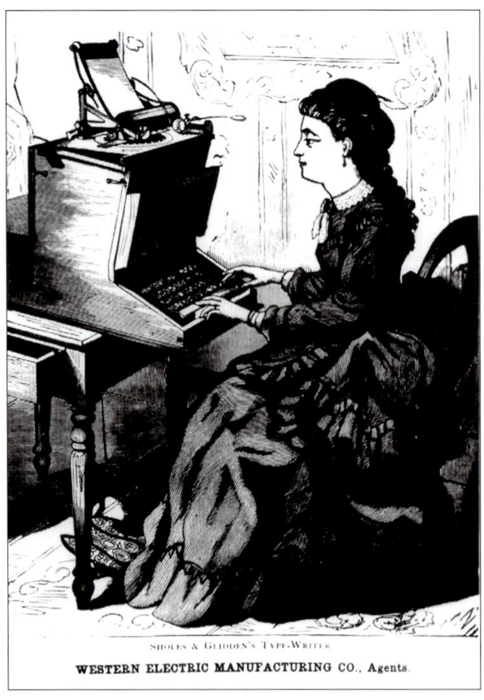

TELEPHONICS: One of the largest employers in Chicagoland was the Western Electric Corporation (now a research division of AT&T). This Western Electric logo profiles an enormous factory that employed 45,000 men and women by 1975. This teletype operator at Western Electric handles a piece of crude yet advanced technology for 1908.

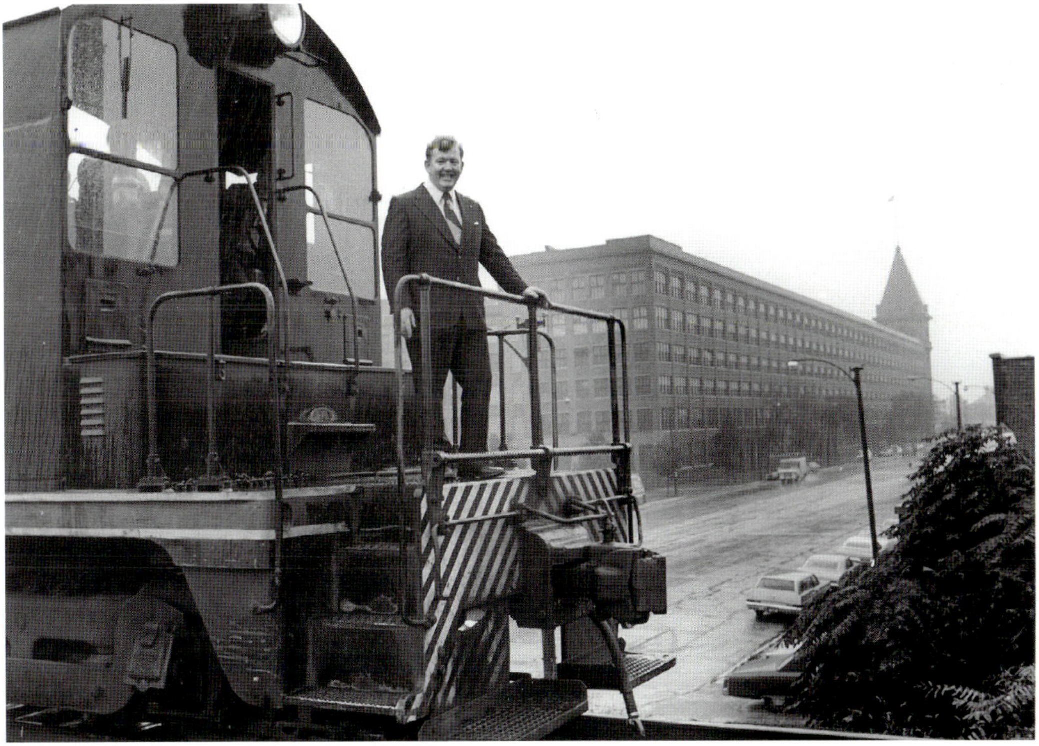

Phone Features:
Western Electric's Bell Laboratory refined telephonics by being the first manufacturer to mass produce vacuum tubes, radar, sonar, telephone party-line capability, and telephone hold functions. They also designed casings for the popular Princess Telephone model. Western Electric advertisements paid particular attention to customer gender and lifestyles.

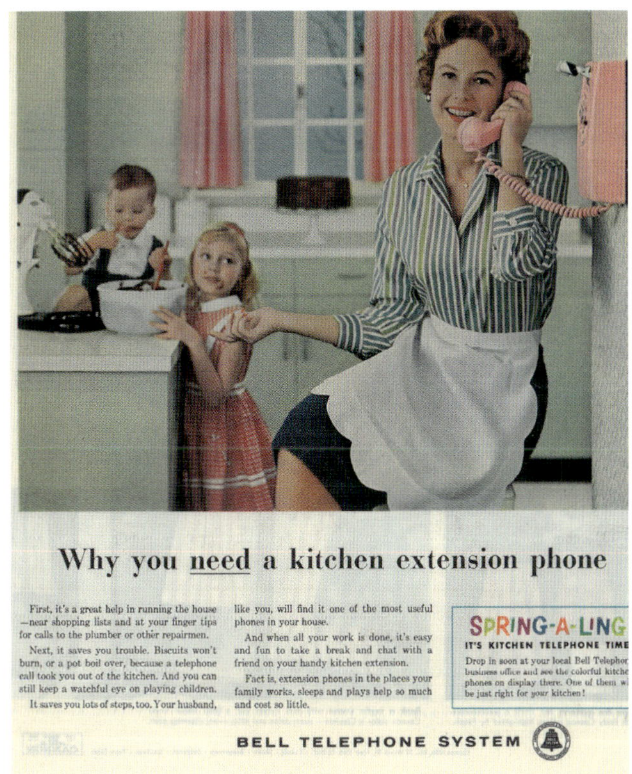

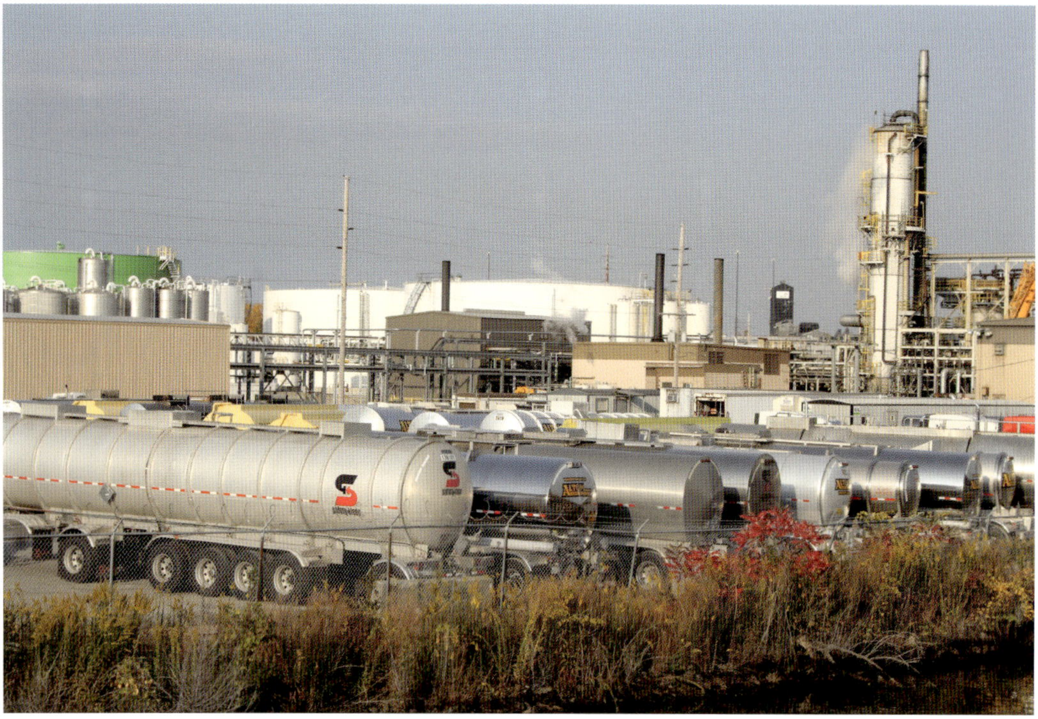

BIG OIL: In 1889 Standard Oil of Northern Indiana was incorporated. Standard not only formulated petroleum, it shipped paint, polyester and other byproducts as well.

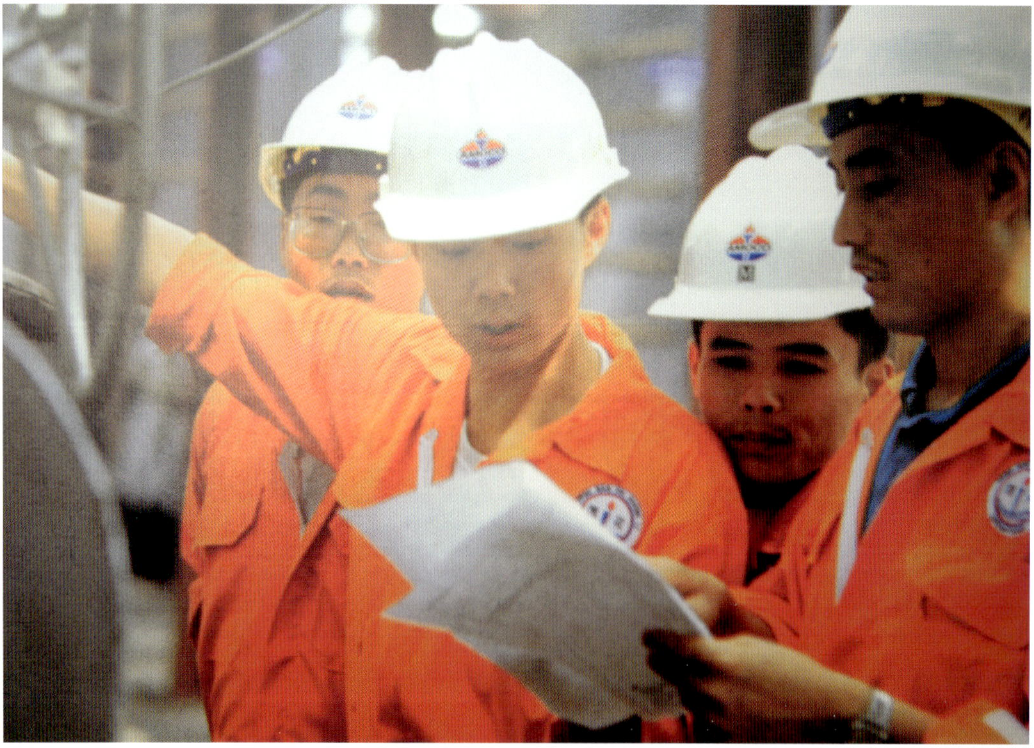

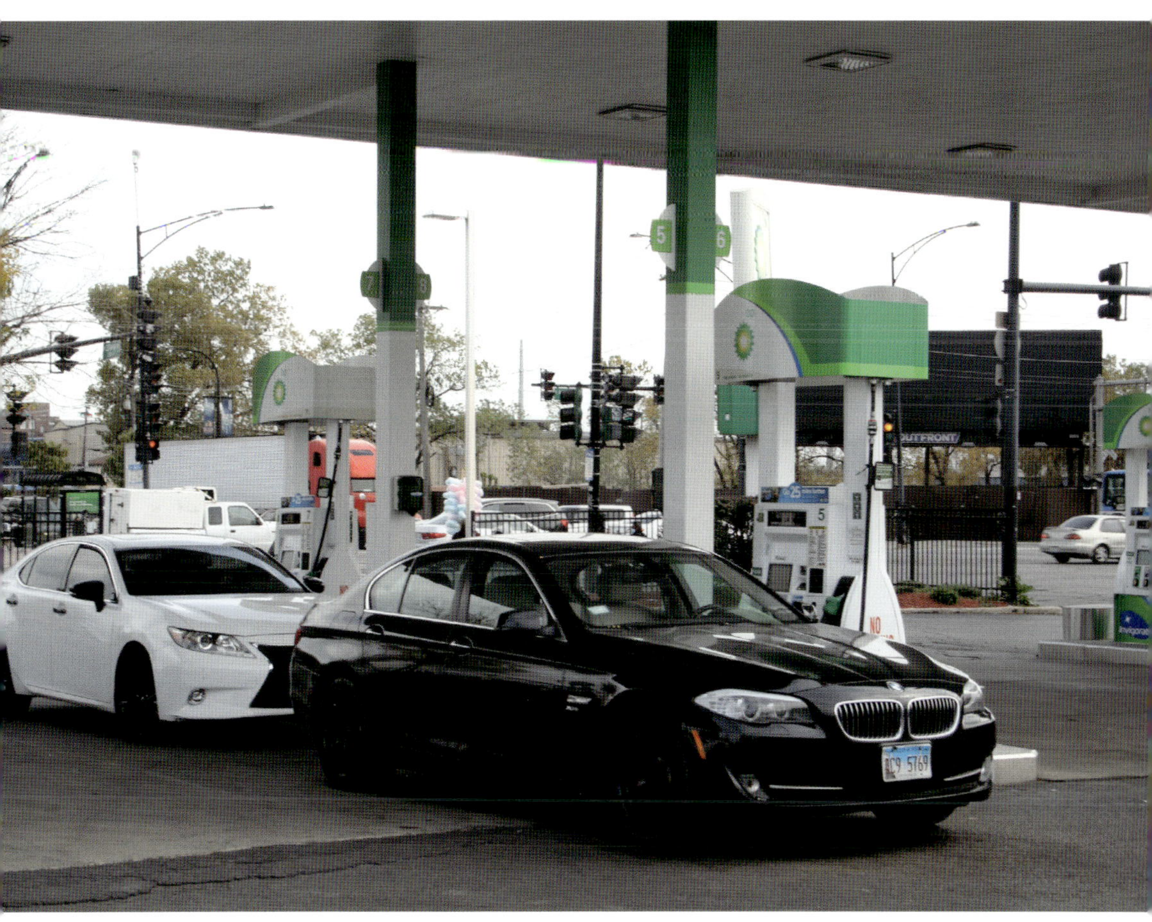

COLLABORATORS AT THE PUMP: Workers from all over the world collaborated and the international headquarters for Amoco was created in Chicago in 1974. By 1998, the BP Corporation took control of the retail pumps in most Midwestern cities and towns. McDonalds also partnered with Amoco for the rights to sell foods in the gas station outlets.

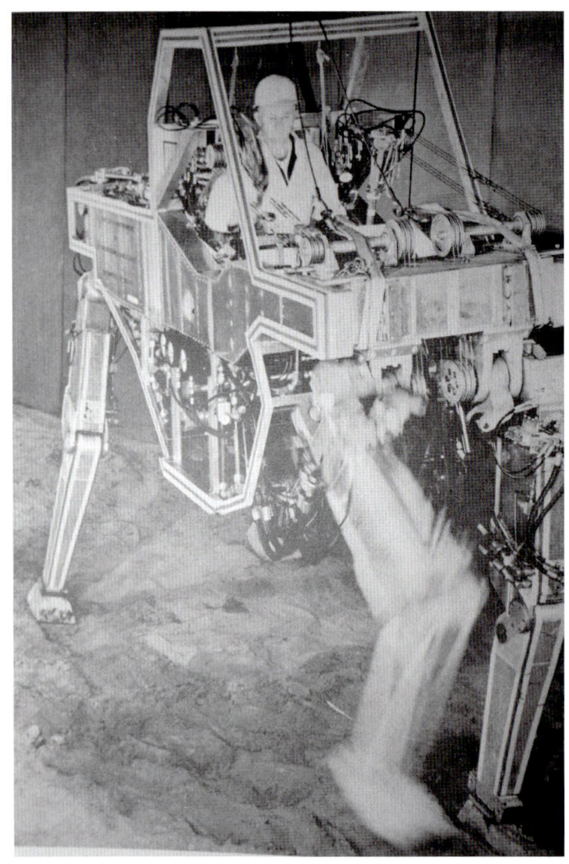

ROBOTICS: Since the 1980s, robots and automation have threated manufacturing jobs in Chicago. Pictured here is a walking machine capable of lifting and pushing hundreds of pounds of industrial materials with the assistance of one person. The input of humans is still vital in this case where operators handle circuit boards for export overseas.

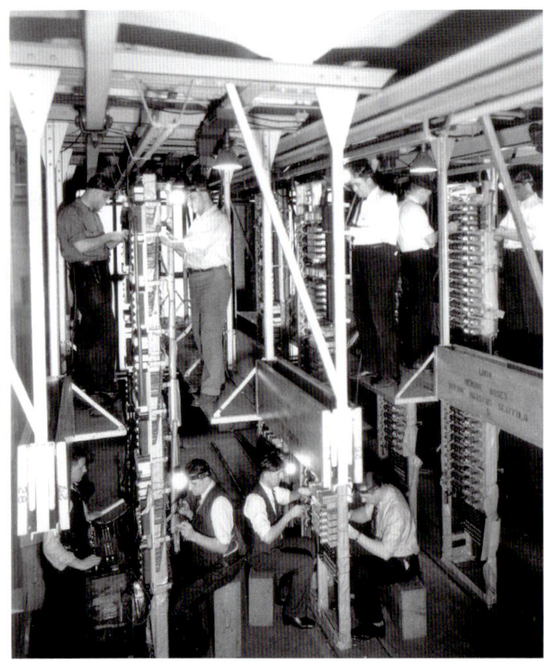

3

FOOD AND BEVERAGES

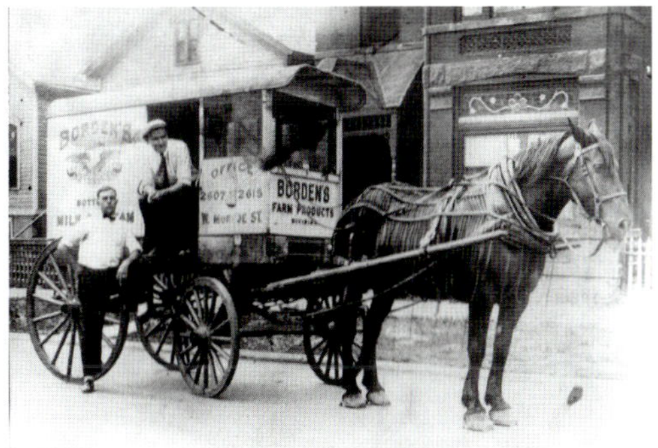

Chicago was, and still is, a key manufacturer of food and drink. Kraft Foods, Morton Salt, Jewel Foods, and Argo Products are a few Chicagoland companies that are top producers in their respective sectors. A micro-example is Vienna Beef LLC, which introduced the Chicago-style hot dog at the World's Columbian Exposition of 1893. Today, Vienna still serves neighborhood outlets offering a meal on a bun for less than $5.00. In 1929, John San Filippo created a nut company in his name. His branded cashews, almonds, macadamias, pecans, and pistachios are now exported to Asian markets from Chicago.

On the subject of beer and brewing, Chicago had several brands that dominated the market for more than seventy-five years: Best Brewery (1885-1961), Peter Hand Inc. (1891-1975), and Monarch Beer (1890-1967). All three beer brands were abundant in many city taverns and local stores, but by 1980, all three producers disappeared. The good news today is that nearly 100 micro-breweries in Illinois are grabbing Midwestern customers away from big name brands. Revolution, Lagunitas, Two Brothers, and Half Acre are beer labels with rising shares of the consumer beer market in Chicago. While a younger generation of entrepreneurs are criticized for letting American industries rust, the local brewing industry in Chicago is experiencing extraordinary growth.

Regarding the fast-food industry, White Castle (1929-the present) is still a profitable Chicago enterprise. If White Castle is the "grandfather" of fast food, McDonald's is the favorite son. Its first outlet in the suburb of Des Plaines, Illinois, made food history in 1955. Today, the "New World Headquarters" moved from the Far West Suburbs to Chicago's downtown.

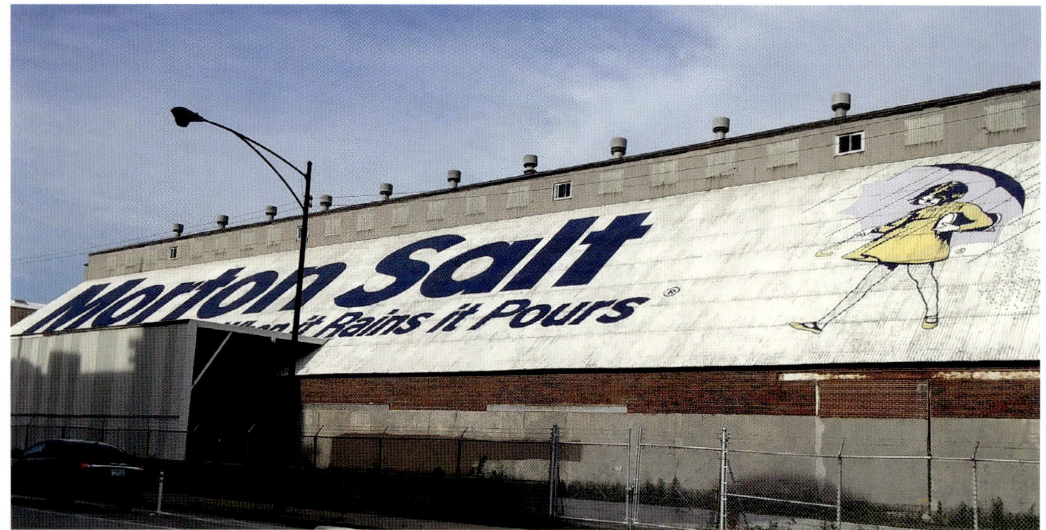

SALT OF THE EARTH: "When it rains, it pours" is a familiar commercial slogan in Chicago. Morton Salt Company was established in 1910. Joy Morton acquired a fleet of lake boats to transport salt from six underground salt mines the company owned. More recently, five solar evaporation plants have been added to the process. Advertising in the 1950s was dominated by radio, TV, and print journalism. Food ads were largely aimed at women since they did the food shopping for their families.

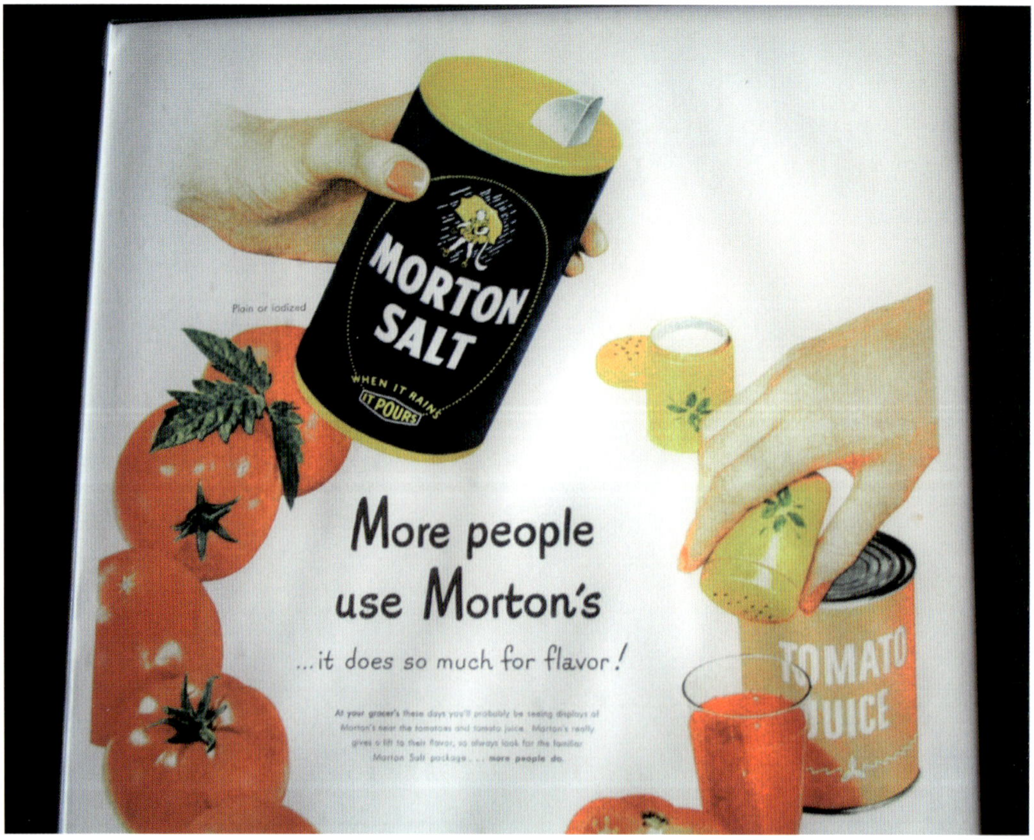

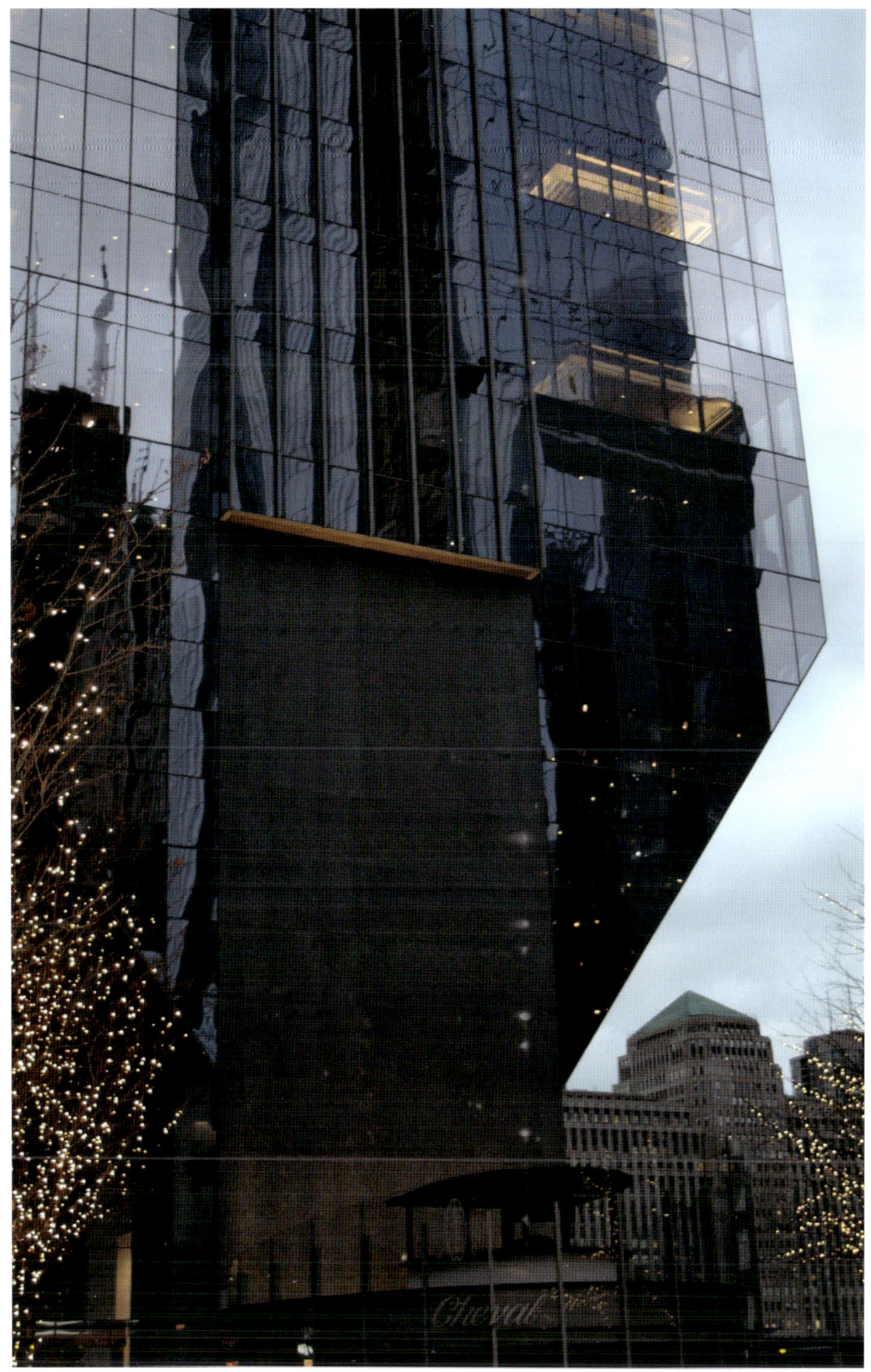

ON THE MOVE: The Morton Salt headquarters moved several times—from Wacker Drive, to Riverside Plaza, and now at River Point. Each move brought more technology and efficiency to making Morton products.

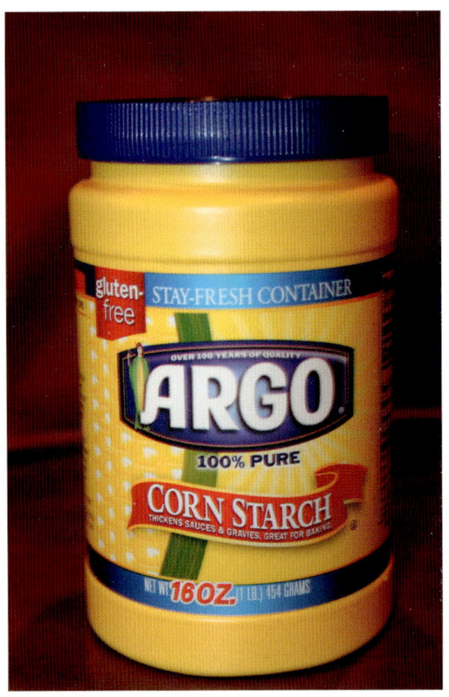

CORNSTARCH AND HISTORY: This name and logo has been on American grocery shelves since 1892. Cornstarch products and their derivatives have been the focus of Argo. Cornstarch is as old as the Egyptian pharaohs, and Roman soldiers used the corn derivative to press their togas. The builder of the Argo central offices kept history in mind by sculpting these friezes onto the company facade.

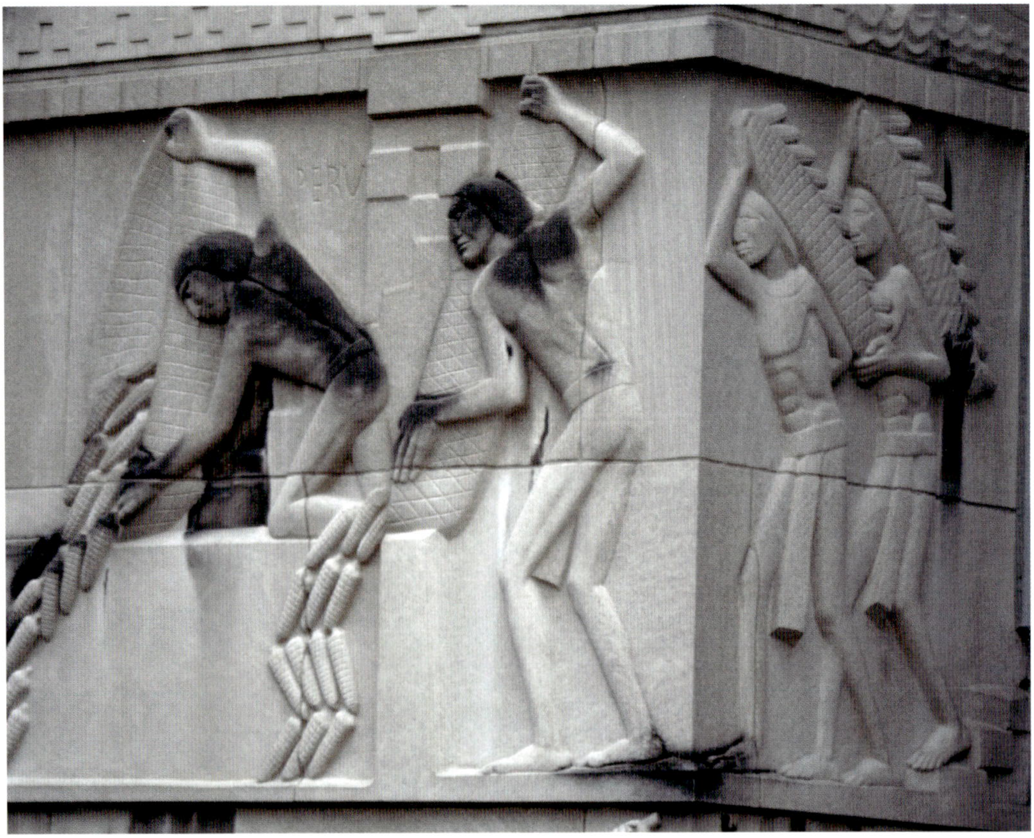

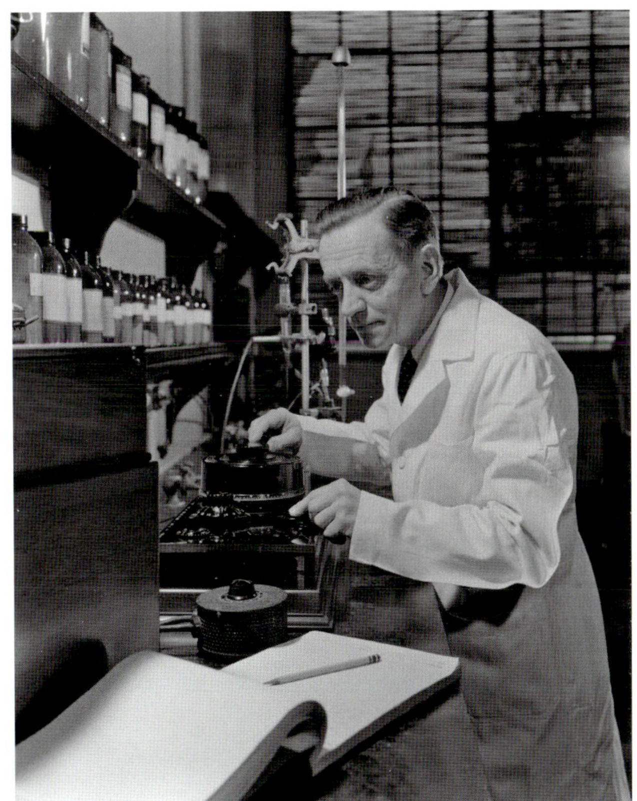

COLLABORATION: Argo lab researchers investigate new applications for corn, tapioca, potatoes, yeast, and vegetable oils. Rather than manufacture all these ingredients, Argo subcontracts with Mazola Incorporated for corn oil, Karo Company for syrup, and Fleischmann Incorporated for yeast. The main Argo factory in Summit, Illinois, takes delivery of these three ingredients and blends them.

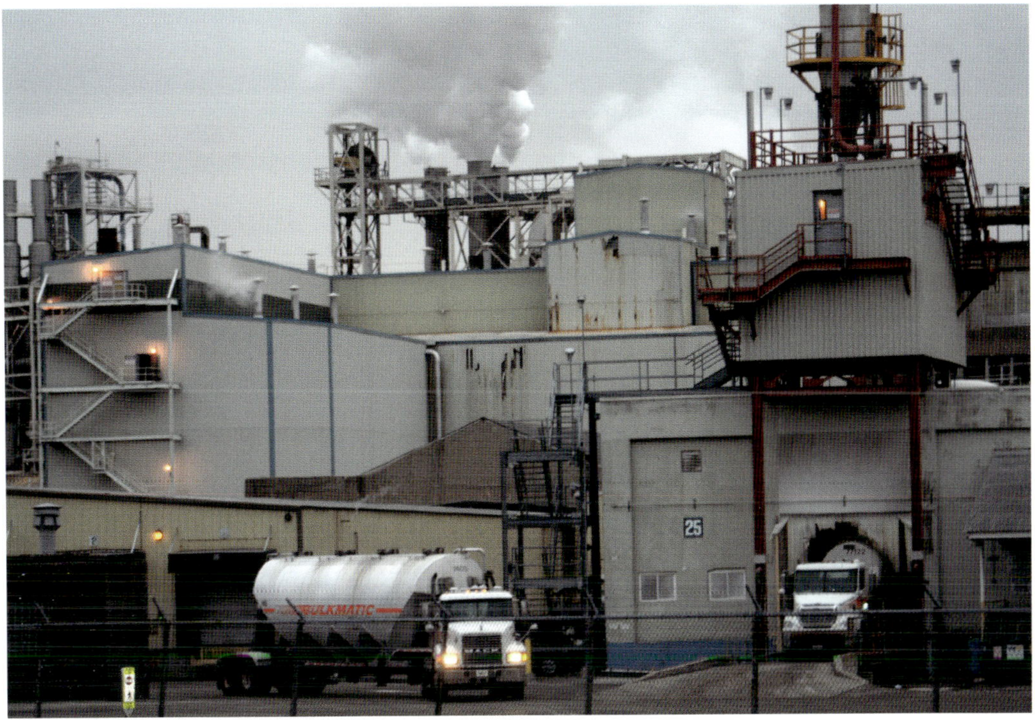

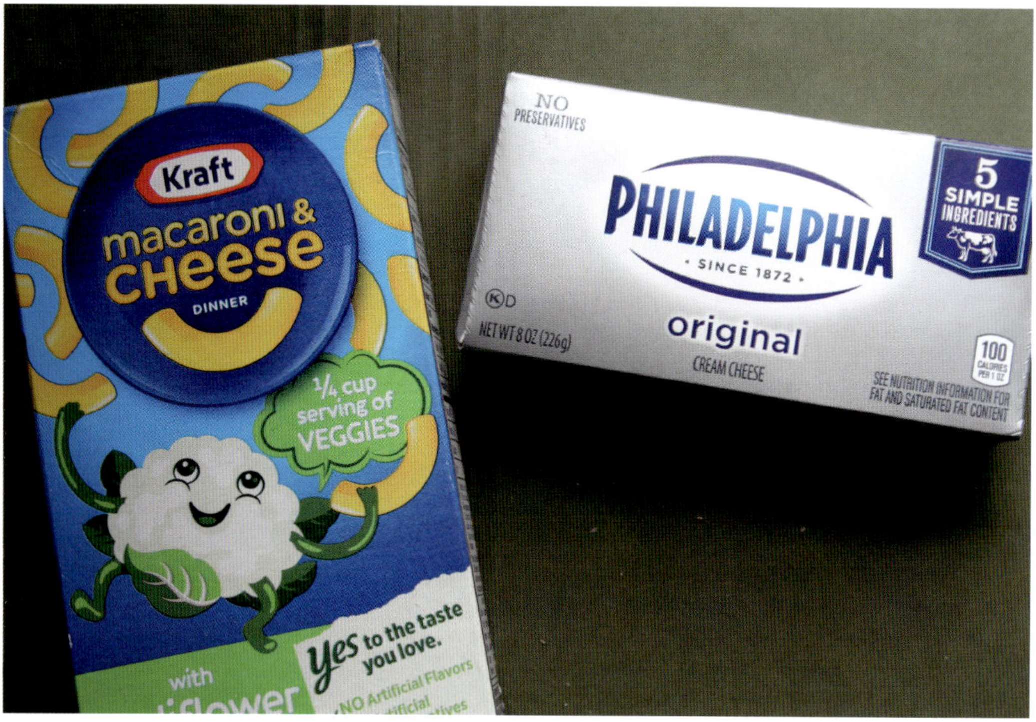

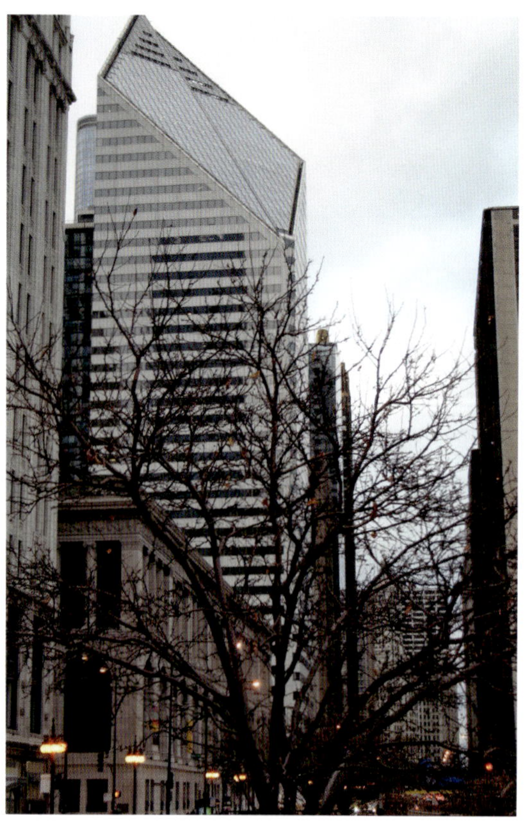

MACARONI AND MORE: In 1903, James Kraft began his career as a door-to-door cheese vendor in Chicago. A few decades later, Kraft created the Velveeta cheese brand, Miracle Whip dressing, macaroni and cheese in a box, and Kool Aid soft drinks. From this tower on Michigan Avenue in Chicago, Kraft planned mergers and buyouts with companies like H. J. Heinz Inc. and Oscar Meyer Foods.

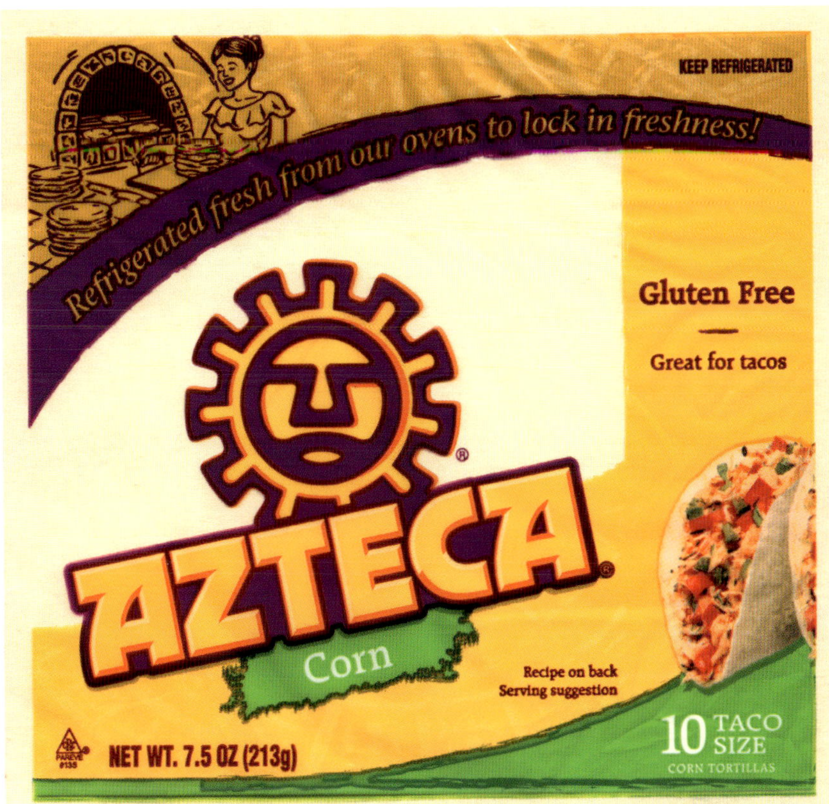

INTERNATIONAL FLAVORS: In 1970, Arthur Velasquez invented refrigerated tortillas with a store shelf-life of ninety days. Supermarkets loved the product, and Azteca Foods Inc. was born. The Azteca kitchen specializes in tortillas that compliment Polish, Italian, Chinese, and Kosher meals. Tortilla salad shells and appetizers are now available on the production line.

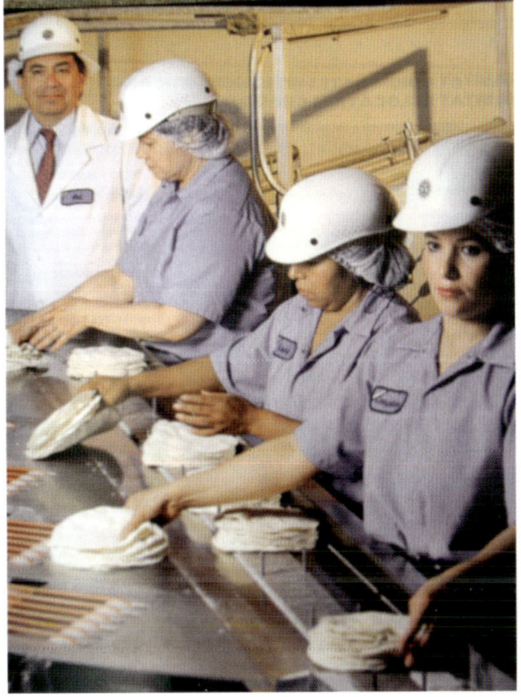

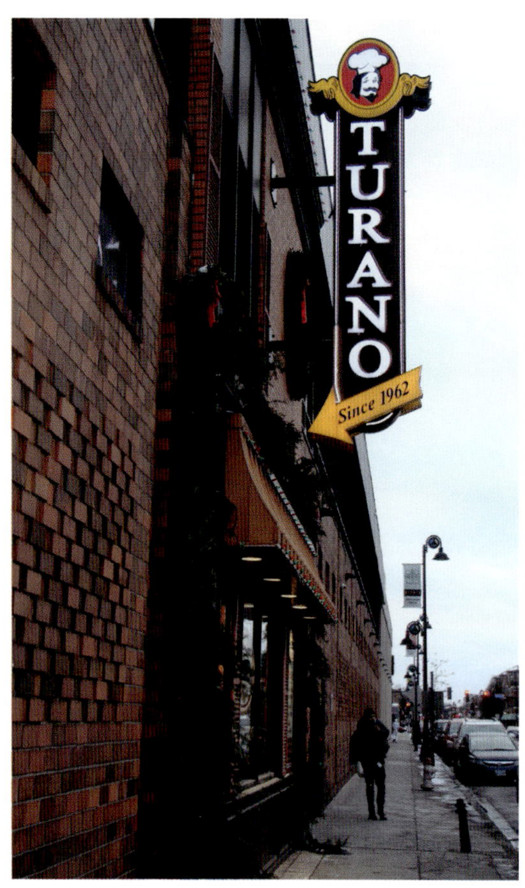

MAKING BREAD: In 1962, Carmen Turano and his two brothers formed a baking company on Chicago's Westside. They made hoagie rolls, ciabatta bread, pizza crust, French bread, and panini loaves on this assembly line.

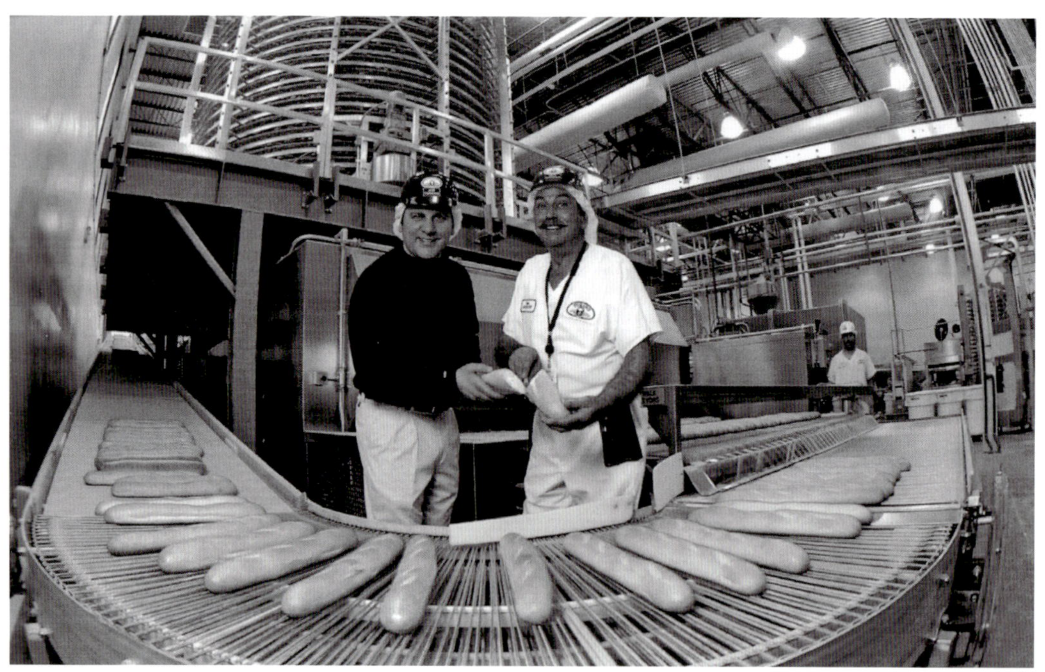

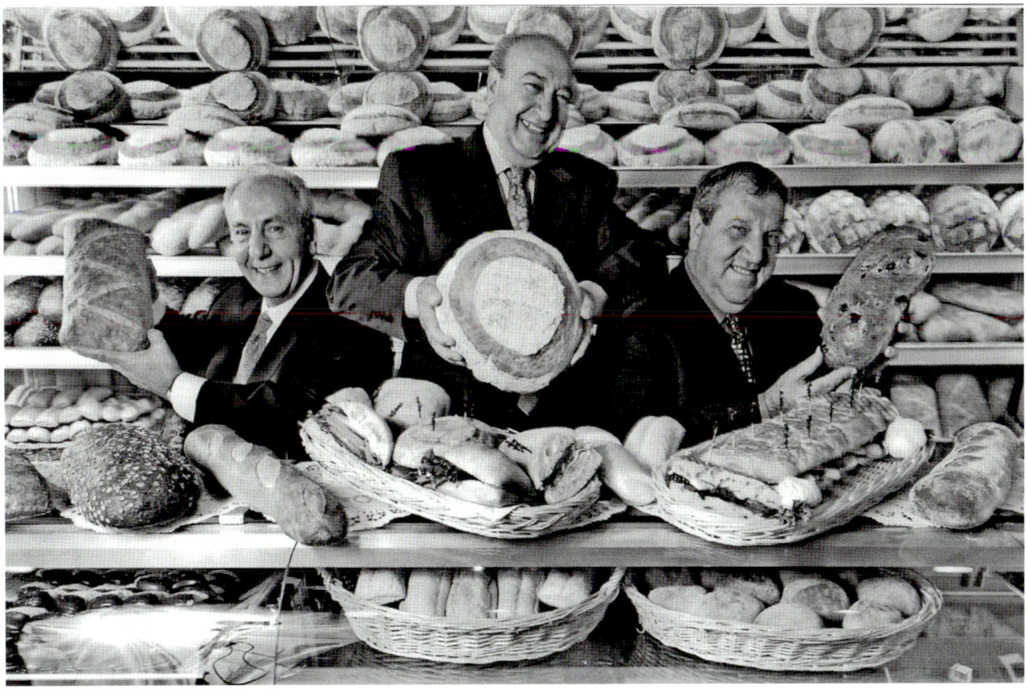

BAKING AND MORE: The Turano family still bakes and distributes products throughout the Midwest region. They are also active with charitable events in the Italian-American community. Currently the Turano outlet store is open six days per week.

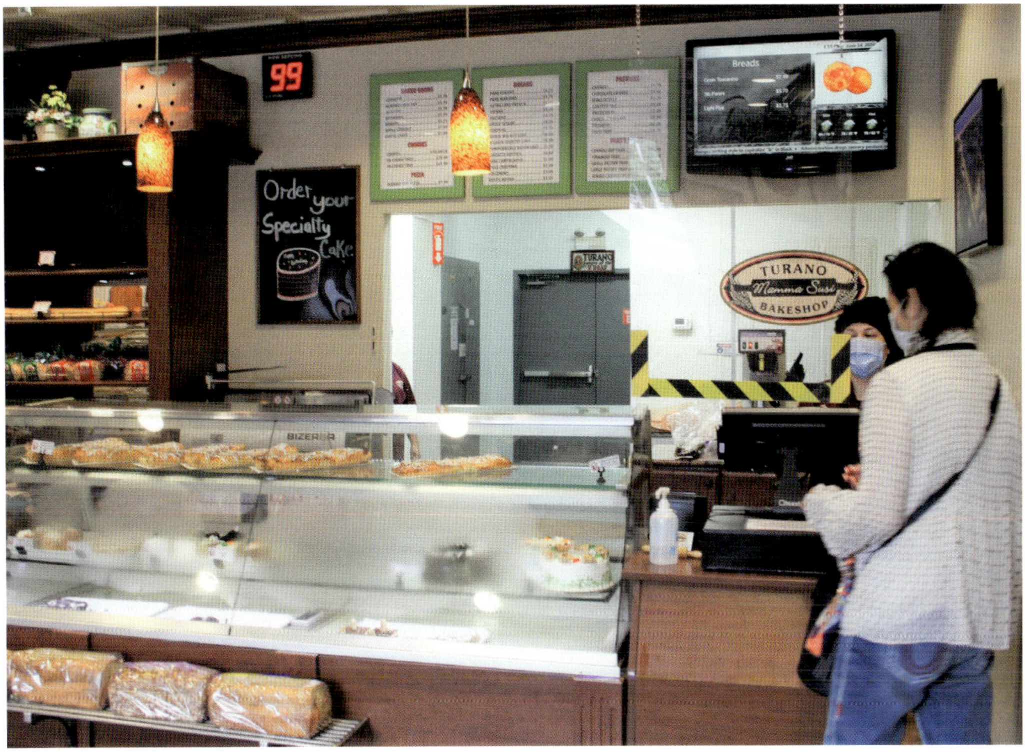

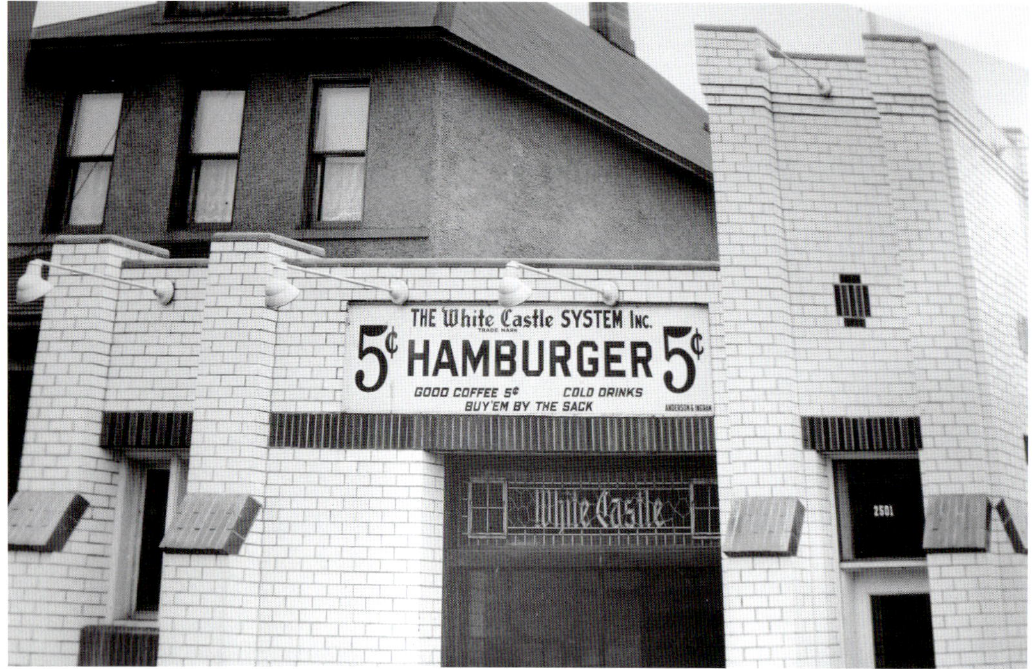

FAST FOOD: In 1929, White Castle Restaurant was the first fast-food chain to reach a hungry market in Chicago. This restaurant on 79th Street sold coffee for a nickel and hamburgers "by the sack." As the second photo indicates, the fast-food concept served busy people on break in Chicago. The assembly line kitchen served all customers in a matter of minutes.

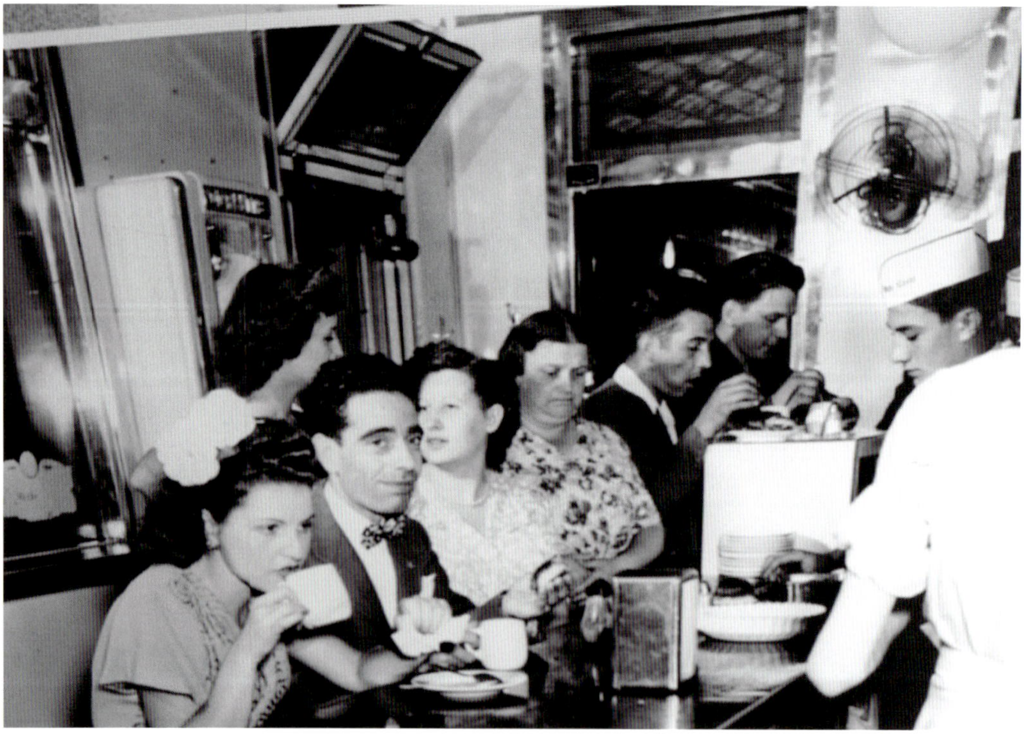

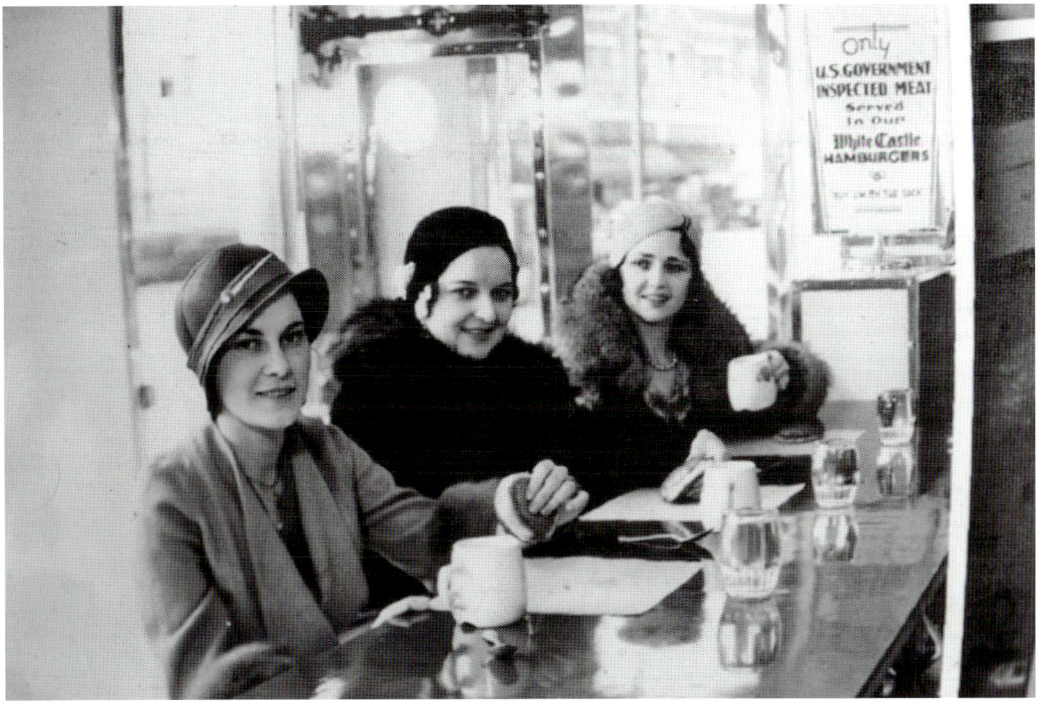

CRAVE CASE: It was fashionable for Chicago "downtown girls" to take lunch at a White Castle Restaurant. Modern brick has replaced the porcelain styled castle of 1929. Today, there are nineteen nearly identical White Castles in the city with just as many in the suburbs.

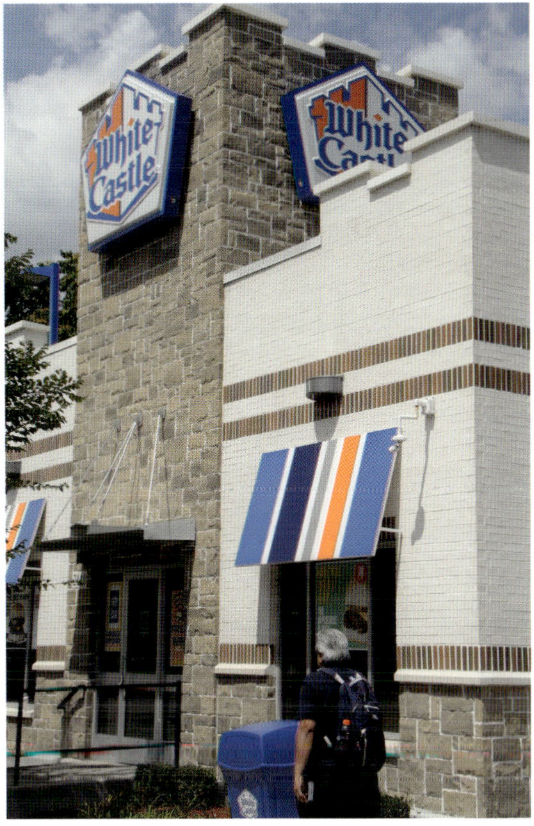

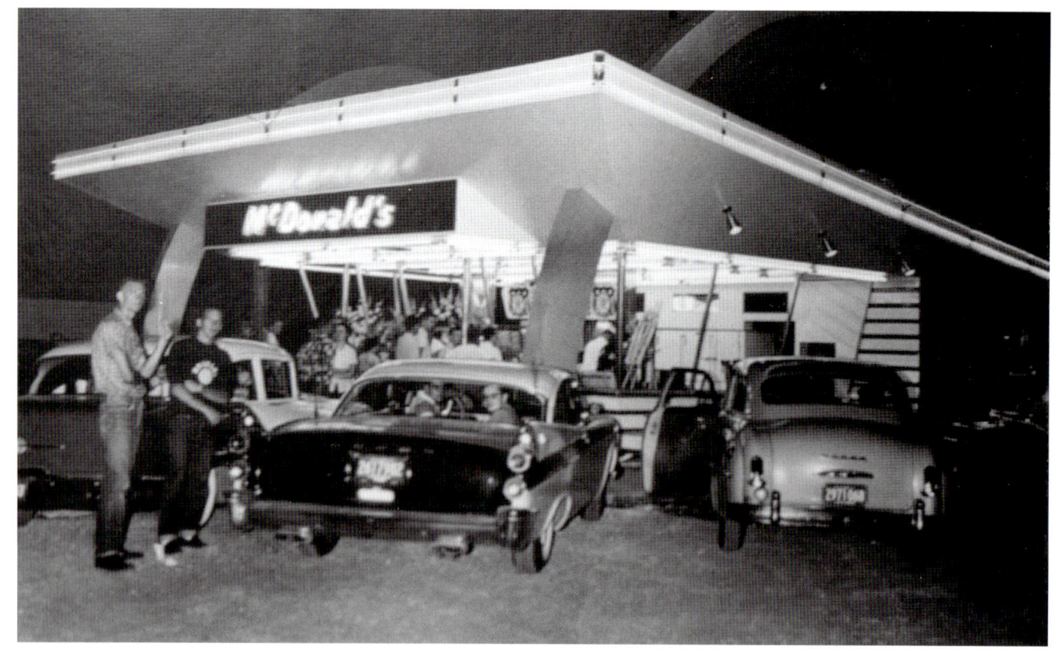

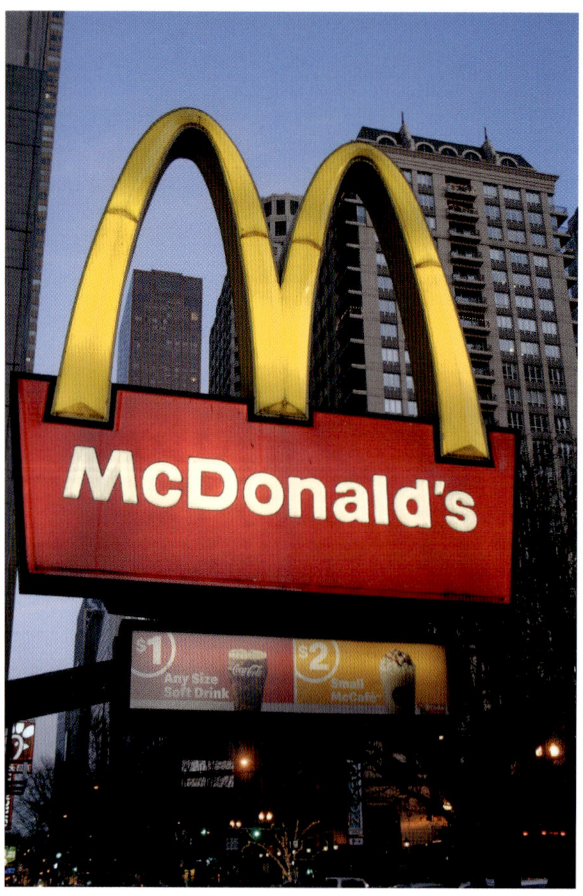

HAMBURGER HEAVEN:
The McDonalds Corporation was born in the Chicago suburb of Des Plaines, Illinois, in 1956. It catered to fast food, car mobility, and youthful tastes. Today, the stores have matured. Sit-down service, urbanity, and even wines have been tried by the stores during years of menu experimentation.

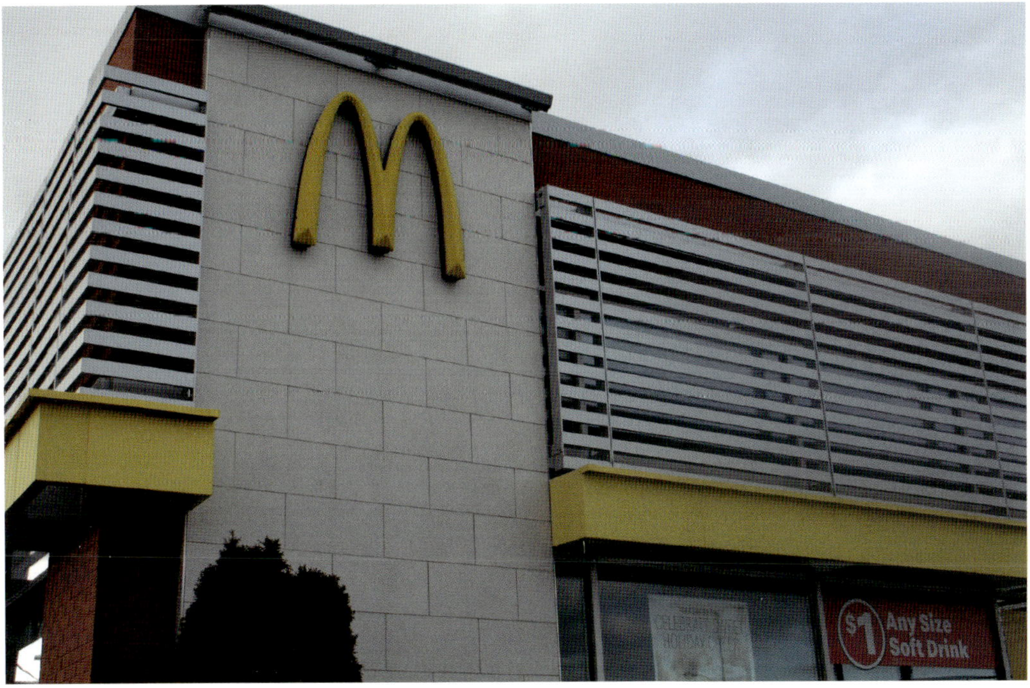

CORPORATISM AND MINIMALISM: Store signs at many new outlets have been reduced to a signature. For example, most of the world knows what goes on beneath the two golden arches. Today, there are thirty-nine stores in central Chicago. Even corporate offices have migrated from the suburbs to downtown. The new McDonalds Hamburger Campus replaced Oprah Winfrey's Harpo Studio in 2018.

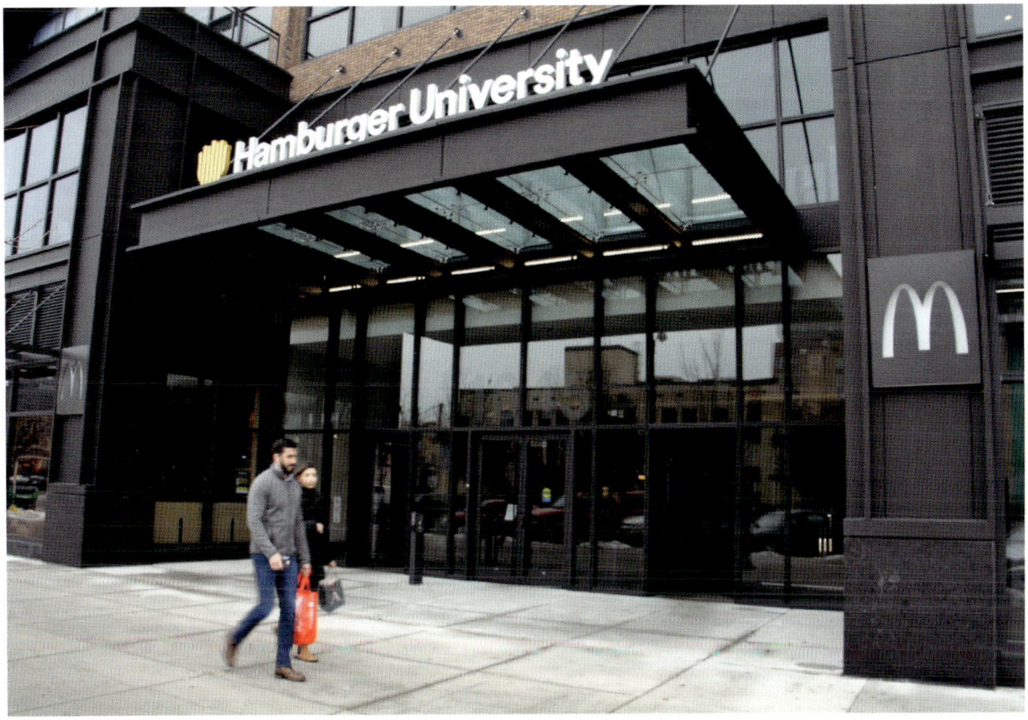

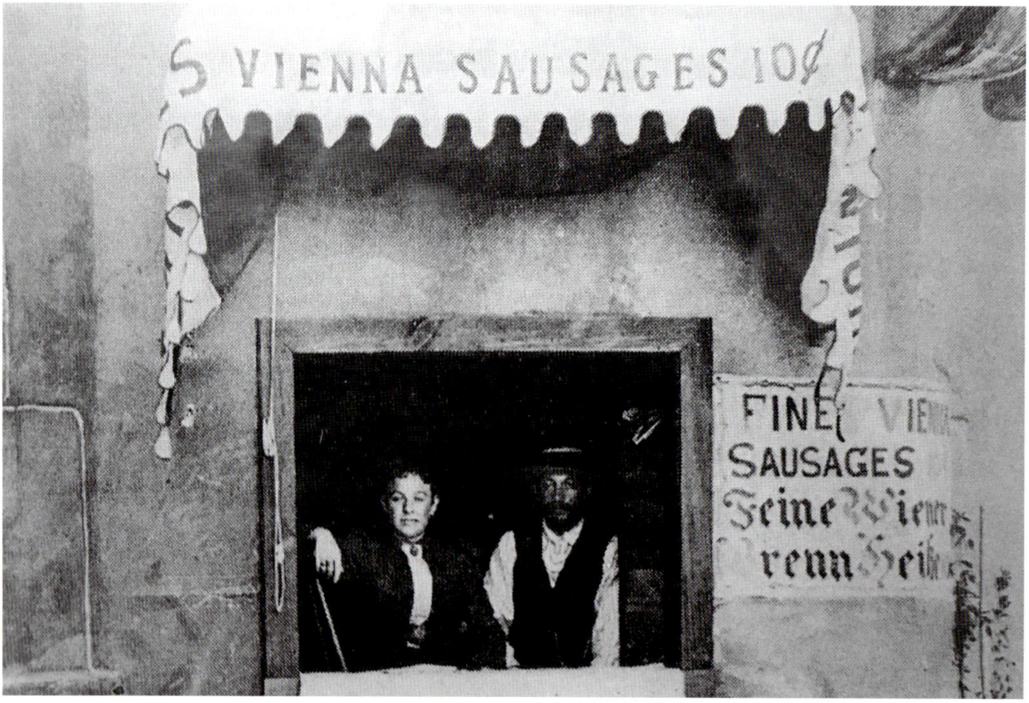

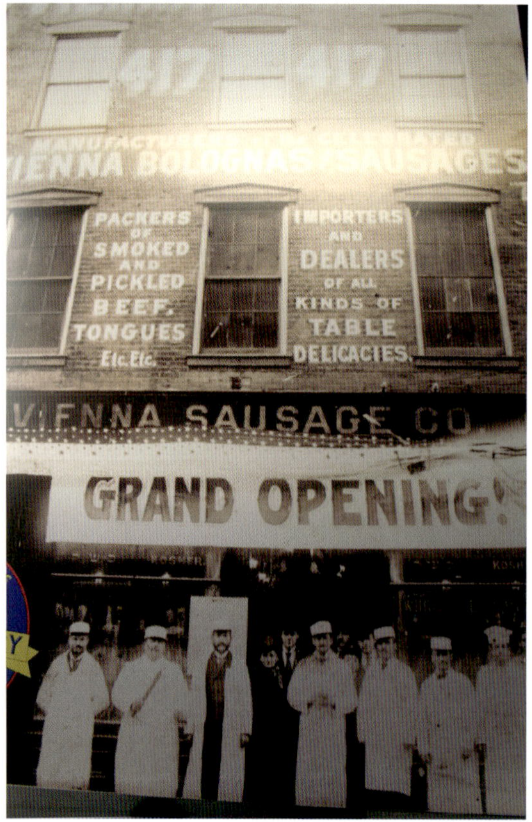

VIENNA COMES TO CHICAGO: In 1893, during the World's Columbian Exposition of Chicago, an all-beef wiener was introduced to hungry crowds. When the expo closed, the Vienna Sausage Company built a store on South Halsted Street, where today the University of Illinois campus is located.

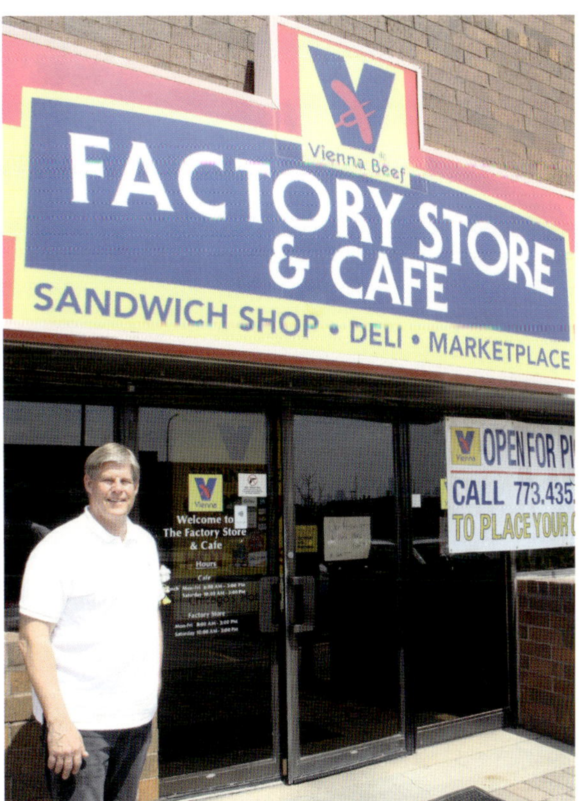

MODERNIZATION AND EXPANSION: Through advertising and customer satisfaction, Vienna Beef grew city-wide. This combination factory and deli serves the city's Northside, while a new outlet is expanding in the Chicago Stockyard neighborhood.

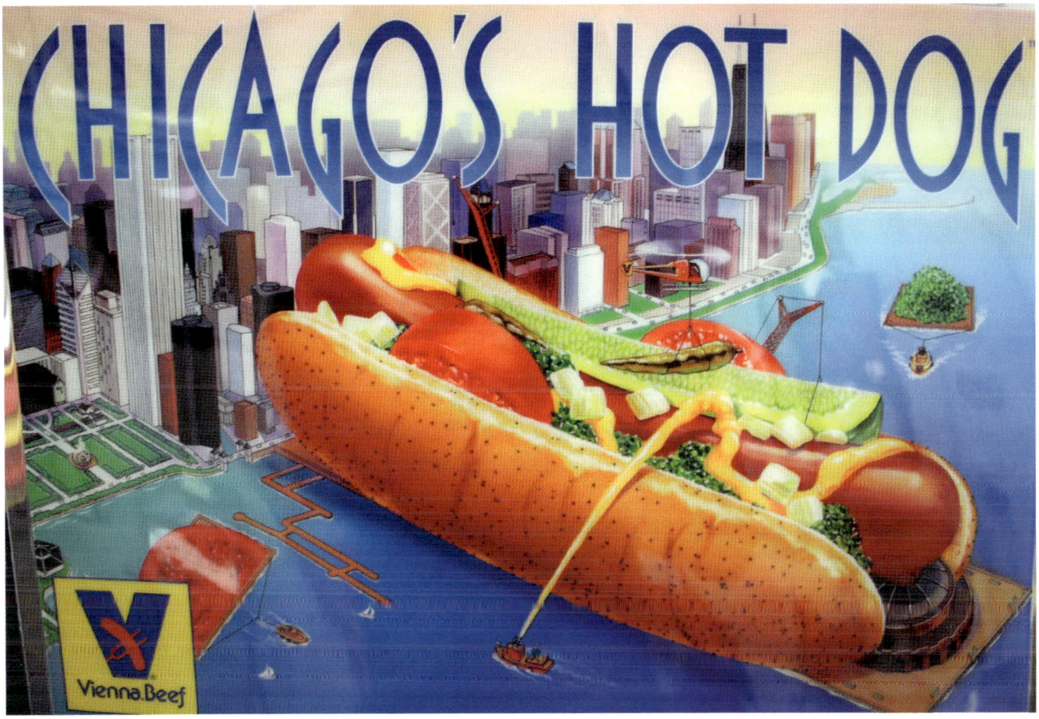

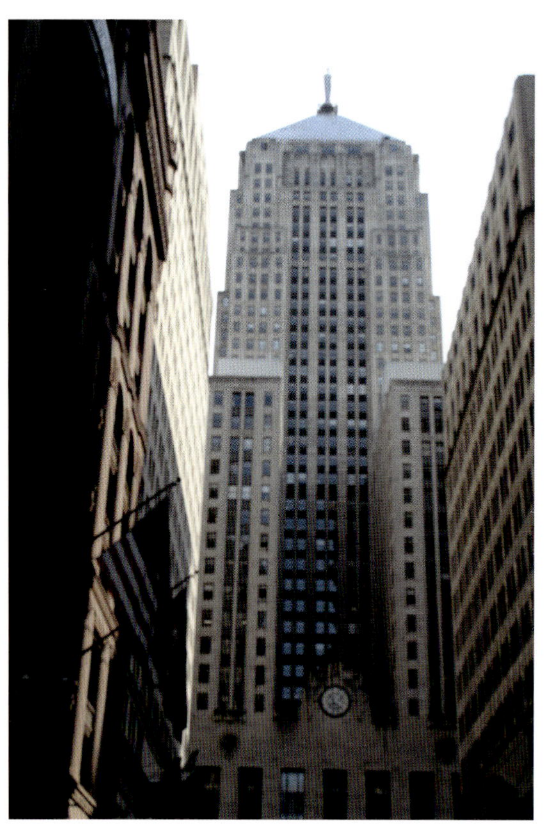

Breadbasket of America: In regard to the past, present, and future of food production, Chicago is an international leader. From seedlings to harvest to trading commodities, the city is an active center. Agricultural giants like Archer, Daniel & Midland, Inc. grow Midwestern grains, Navistar tractors harvest crops, and the Chicago Board of Trade deals in agricultural commodities as affected by price, climate, and competition. The shopper in this photo grabs a bag of Jay's Potato Chips, manufactured on Chicago's Southside for more than seventy-five years.

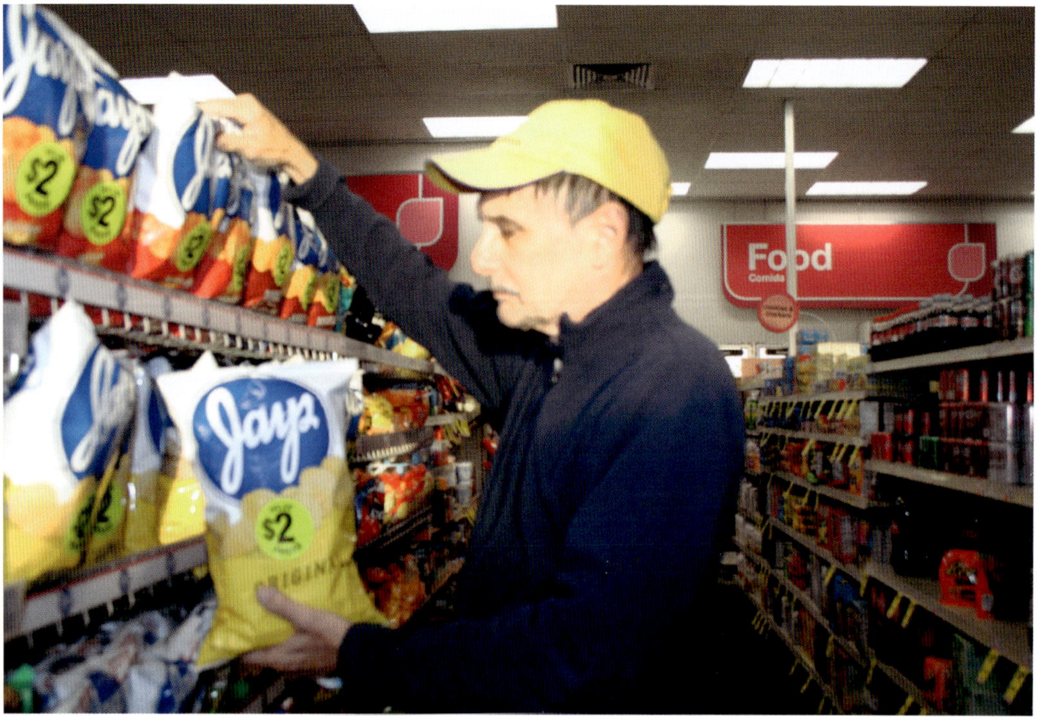

4

Printing and Publishing

For many decades Chicago has led the nation in the field of printing and commercial publishing. Some of the earliest firms include: R. R. Donnelley Co. (1864), Rand McNally Inc.(1868), Cuneo Press (1890), Scott Foresman Co. (1896), and the Lakeside Press (1897).

Chicago was a go-to city in regard to the printing industry. Paul Gehl, with the *Encyclopedia of Chicago*, states that "by the end of the 20th century, four of the 10 largest printing companies in the world were headquartered in Metropolitan Chicago." Mr. Gehl further reports that "there were 2,100 printing establishments in the Chicago industry employing close to 100.000 workers" engaged in printing, sales, and distribution jobs.

One factor that nurtured the printing business was mass transportation. Chicago was a hub of conjoining railroads that delivered to printing houses. Chicago also had many immigrant artisans who were experts in the printing and publishing fields.

Print products with a Chicago focus in the last century included newspapers, magazines, mail order catalogs, textbooks, religious literature, and phonebooks, all aimed at household consumers. Chicago added its own specialties like map production. The first U.S. national highway atlas was introduced by the Rand McNally Company in 1924. This marked the beginning of popular vacation travel mapping. In addition to flat maps, Chicago was a major producer of globes. The Replogle Company was determined to place a world globe as a centerpiece in every American home. To this end, Replogle continues today.

The Chicago Tribune Corporation exists in a very competitive news industry today. News delivered by cellphones and personal computers attracts consumers in a crowded market. While the Tribune has sold off its radio and TV media, their core business has been in newsprint since 1847. The *Chicago Defender* newspaper found its niche among black readers in 1905. The *Defender* is still a voice for black civil rights and social justice but is now largely an online news format.

Chicago has its own publishing stars. Mortimer Adler's *Great Books* collection based at the University of Chicago was described as "the world's great ideas on a single shelf." Dr. William Gray, also of the University of Chicago, wrote the *Dick and Jane* elementary school book series published by the Scott Foresman Company. Both Adler's idea-collection and Gray's school books found a place in middle-American homes. These projects were formative to several generations of readers, and they are examples of the Chicago ideal of "literacy for all."

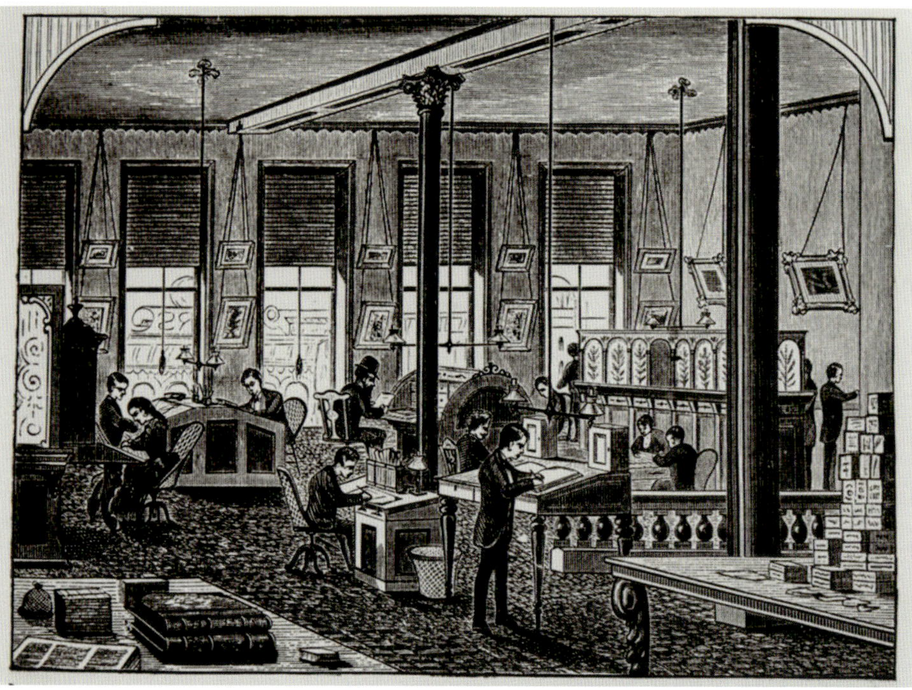

THE PRINTING PRESS: In 1871, Rand McNally started book publishing of all kinds. Their *Street Map & Highway Atlas* became their most popular product. Rand McNally needed thousands of men and women to print, bind, and assemble thousands of paperback and hardcover books.

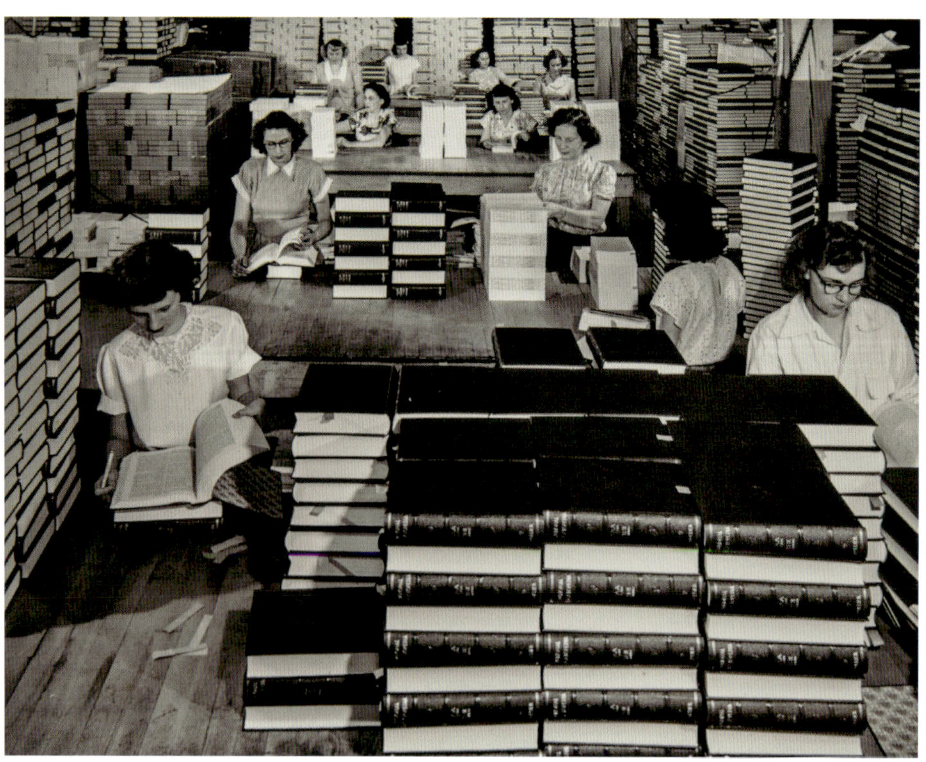

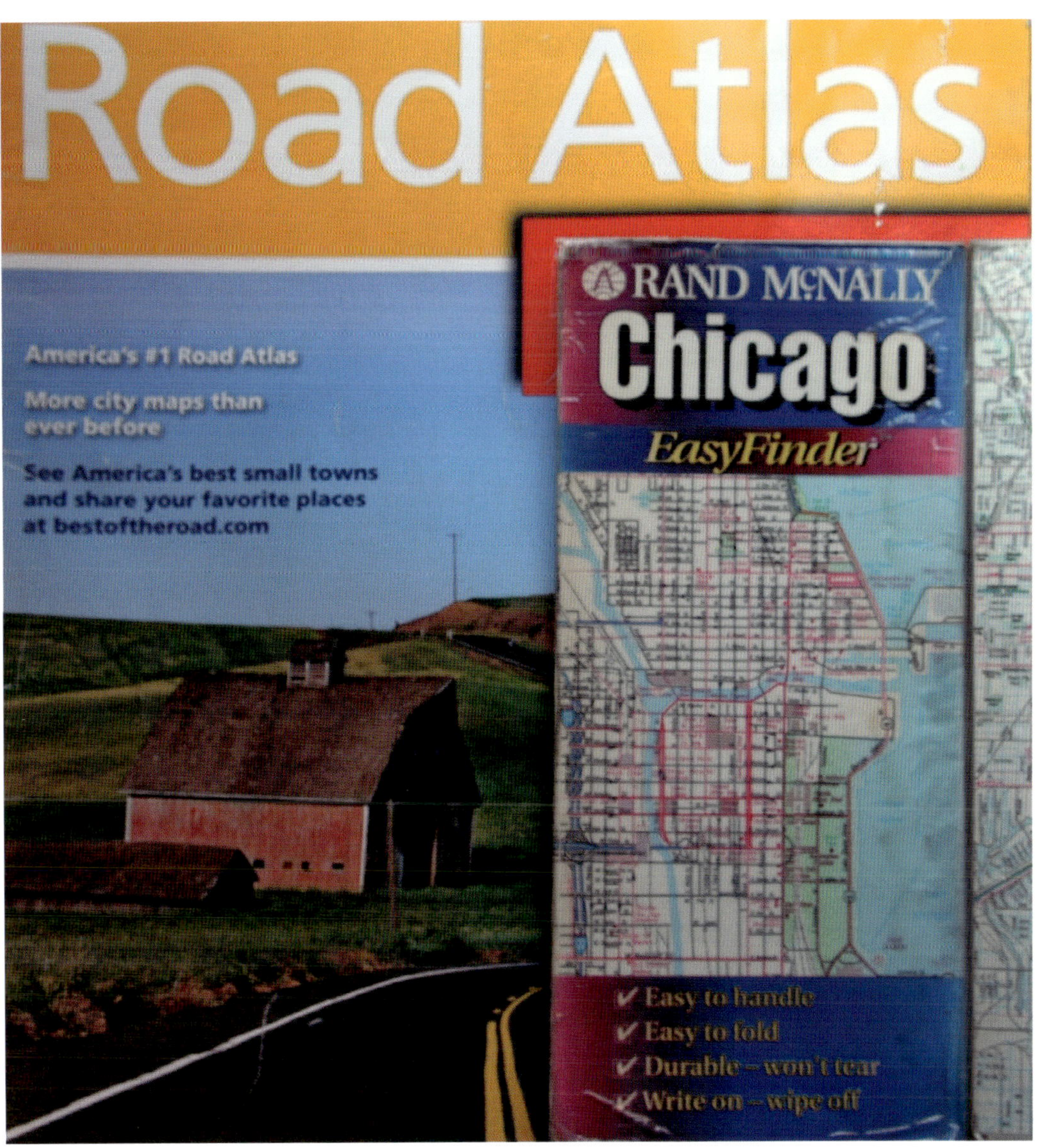

HIGHWAY SURGE: In 1924, Rand McNally Company printed the first United States national highway map. Today, motorists can buy the maps in paper or digital form for travel convenience.

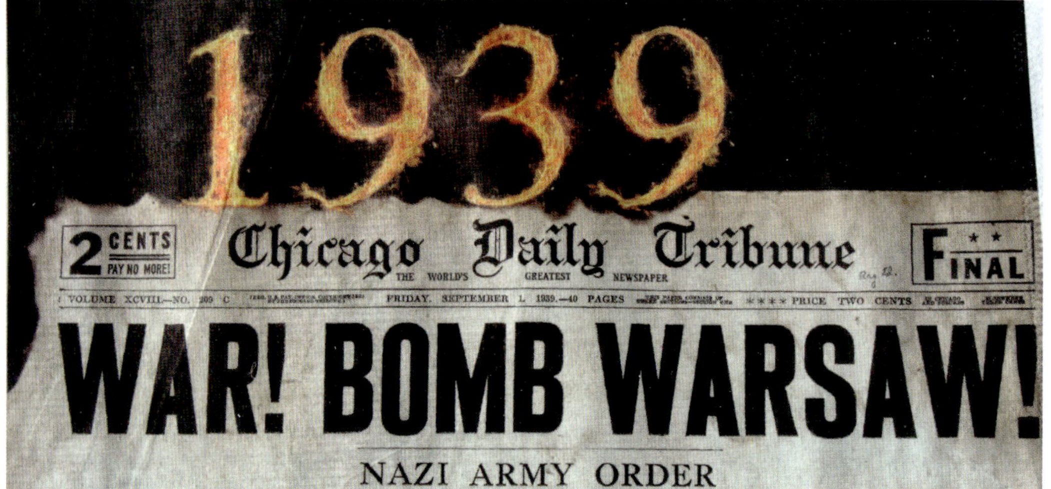

1939

2 CENTS PAY NO MORE!

Chicago Daily Tribune

THE WORLD'S GREATEST NEWSPAPER

FINAL

VOLUME XCVIII.—NO. 209 C FRIDAY, SEPTEMBER 1, 1939.—40 PAGES PRICE TWO CENTS

WAR! BOMB WARSAW!

NAZI ARMY ORDER

BERLIN, Sept. 1 (Friday) (A.P.)—Adolf Hitler today ordered the German army to meet force with force. His order of the day to the army read:

"The Polish state has rejected my efforts to establish neighborly relations, and instead has appealed to weapons. Germans in Poland are victims of a bloody terror, driven from house and home. A series of border violations unbearable for a great power show that the Poles no longer are willing to respect the German border.

"To put an end to these insane incitations, nothing remains but for me to meet force with force from now on. The German army will conduct a fight for honor and the right to the life of the resurrected German people with firm determination.

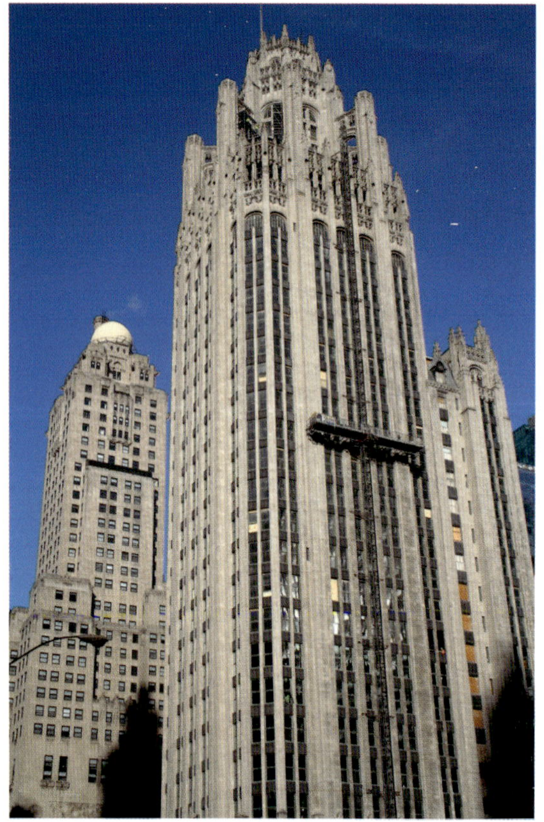

CHICAGO TRIBUNE: Since 1847, the Tribune Company has delivered news on world events and city news. The neo-gothic skyscraper is the corporate landmark for the newspaper, but this tower will soon be converted to private condominiums. The Tribune Media Company will continue to publish and broadcast news into the next century.

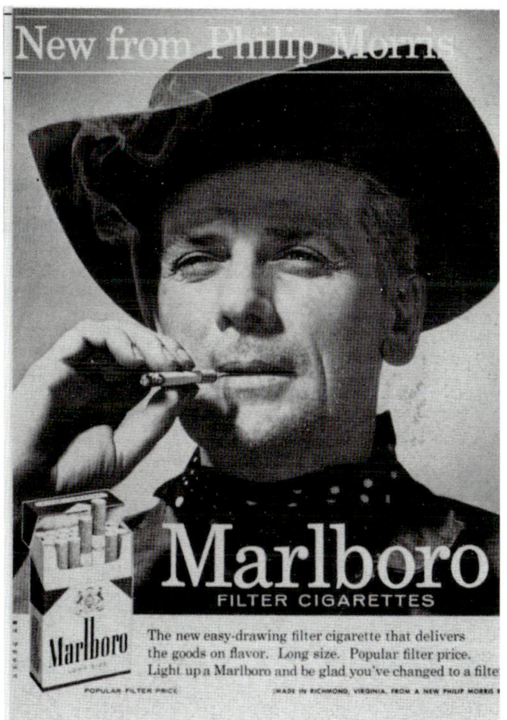

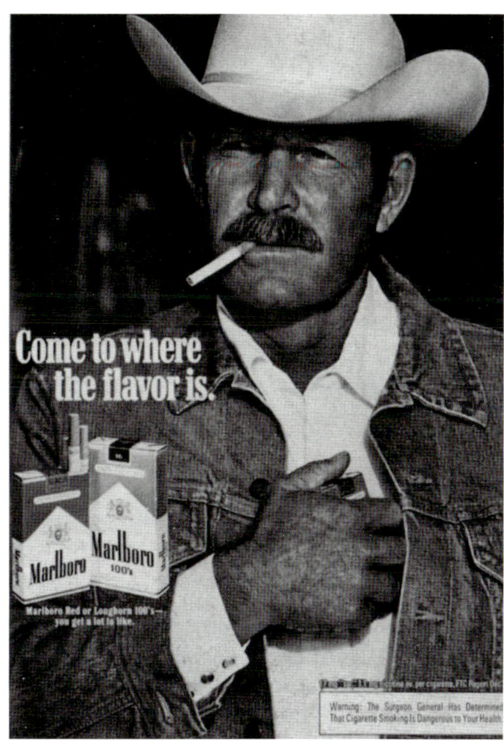

COWBOYS AND CARTOONS: The Leo Burnett Agency has been creating advertising in Chicago since its inception in 1935. Burnett writers created clever characters like Charlie the Tuna, the Jolly Green Giant, the Maytag Man, and Tony the Tiger to promote specific products. Featured here are two images of the Marlboro Men in contrast from 1955 and 1984. Today, the Burnett headquarters operates out of a modernist Chicago skyscraper on Wacker Drive. In addition, seventy-one offices in the USA and abroad are occupied by Burnett ad talent.

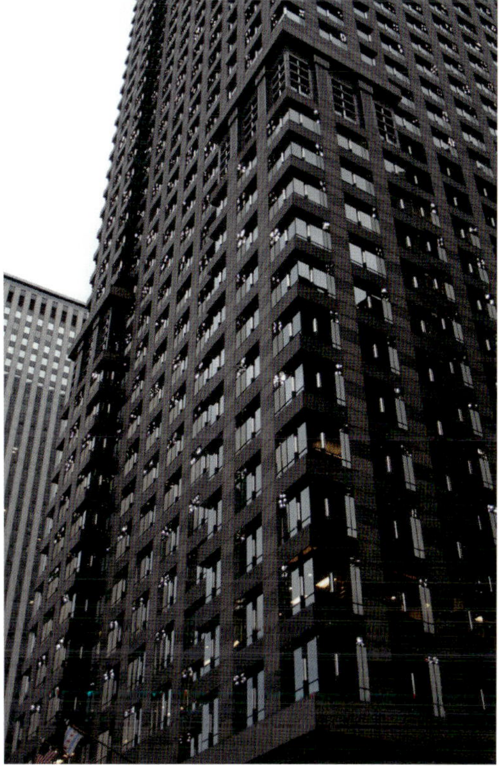

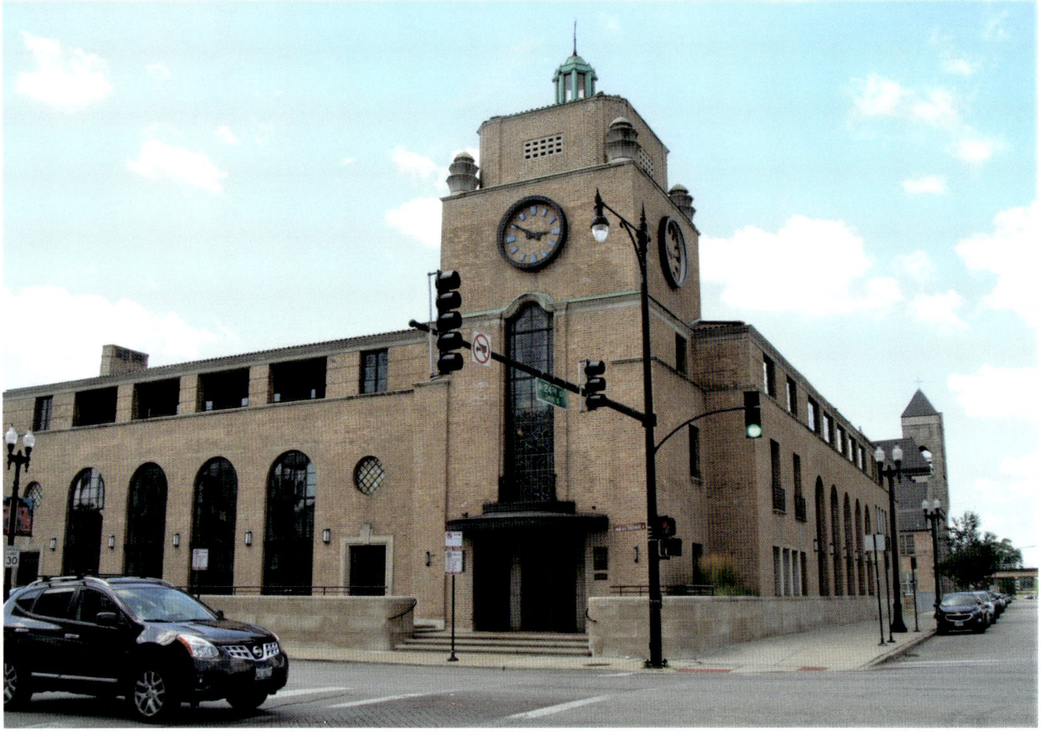

THE DEFENDER: The *Chicago Daily Defender* is a voice for minorities. Founded in 1905 in a former Jewish Synagogue, the *Defender* building is today designated a Chicago Landmark. The mission of the newspaper continues in support of African-American civil rights. The editorial offices moved to Detroit, Michigan, in 2010, but the mission of the *Defender* has rarely wavered.

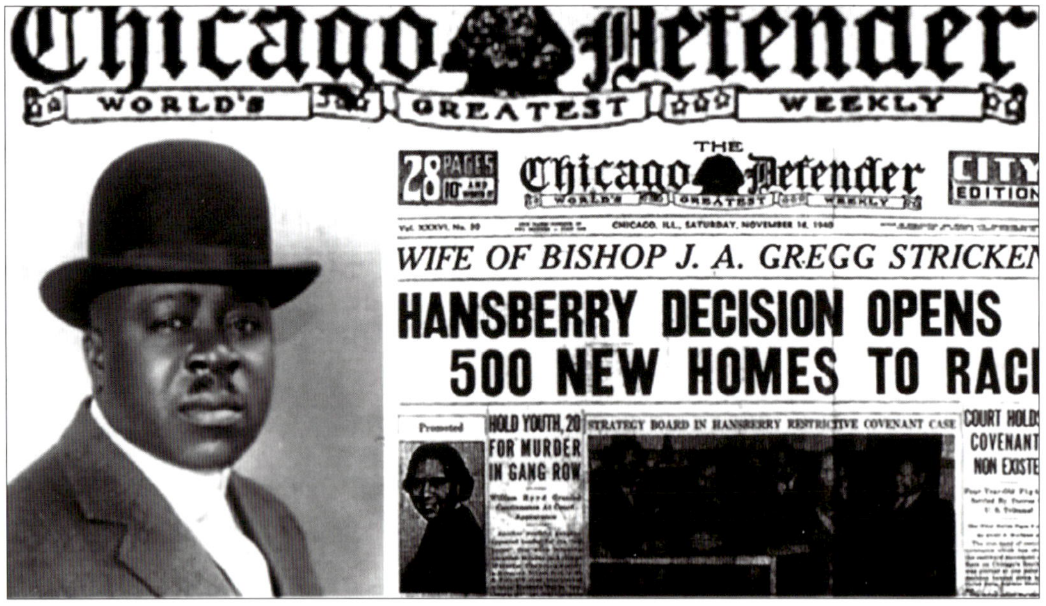

Chicago Defender

WORLD'S GREATEST WEEKLY

28 PAGES

THE Chicago Defender

WORLD'S GREATEST WEEKLY

CITY EDITION

WIFE OF BISHOP J. A. GREGG STRICKEN

HANSBERRY DECISION OPENS 500 NEW HOMES TO RAC

Promoted

HOLD YOUTH, 20 FOR MURDER IN GANG ROW

STRATEGY BOARD IN HANSBERRY RESTRICTIVE COVENANT CASE

COURT HOLDS COVENANT NON EXISTE

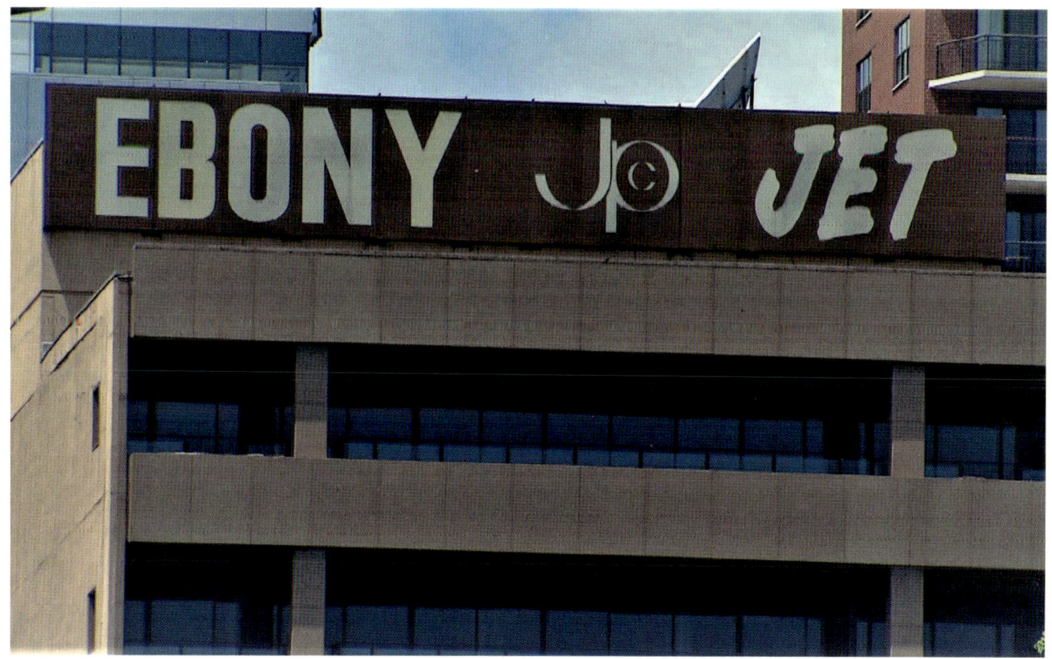

EBONY: *Ebony and Jet* magazines focus on African Americans in the news. John H. Johnson created a huge enterprise on Michigan Avenue in Chicago based on two publications and a variety of hair care products. As of 2016, the new buyer of Johnson Publications is the Ebony Media Corporation. Their focus is still on African-American political figures, entertainers, athletes, authors, and outstanding black personalities today.

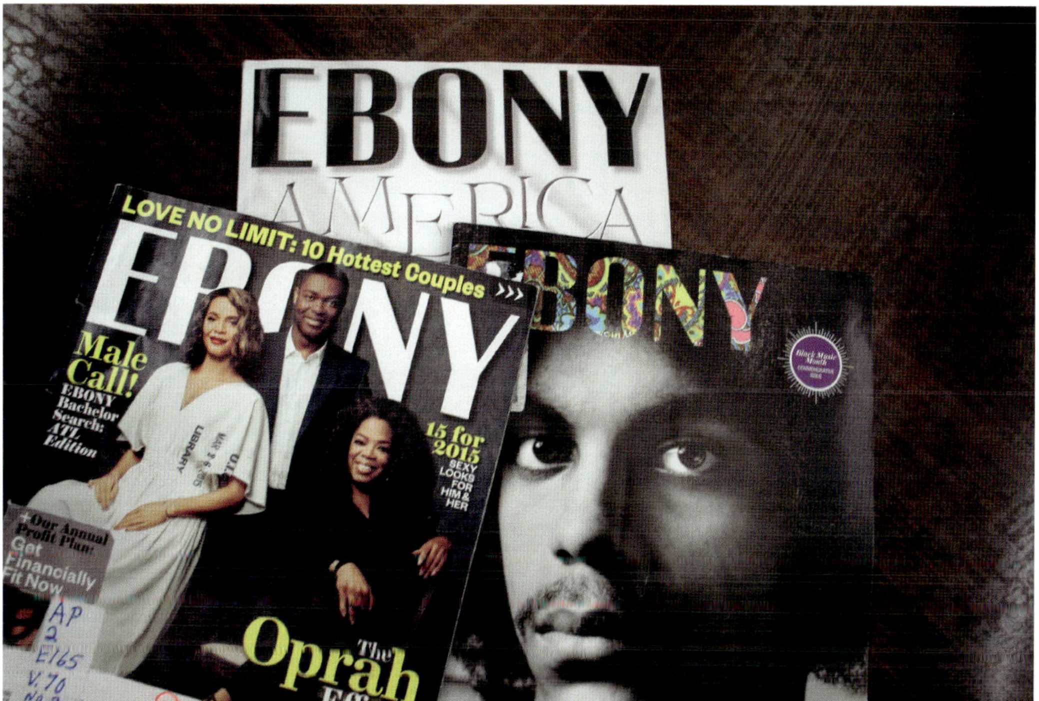

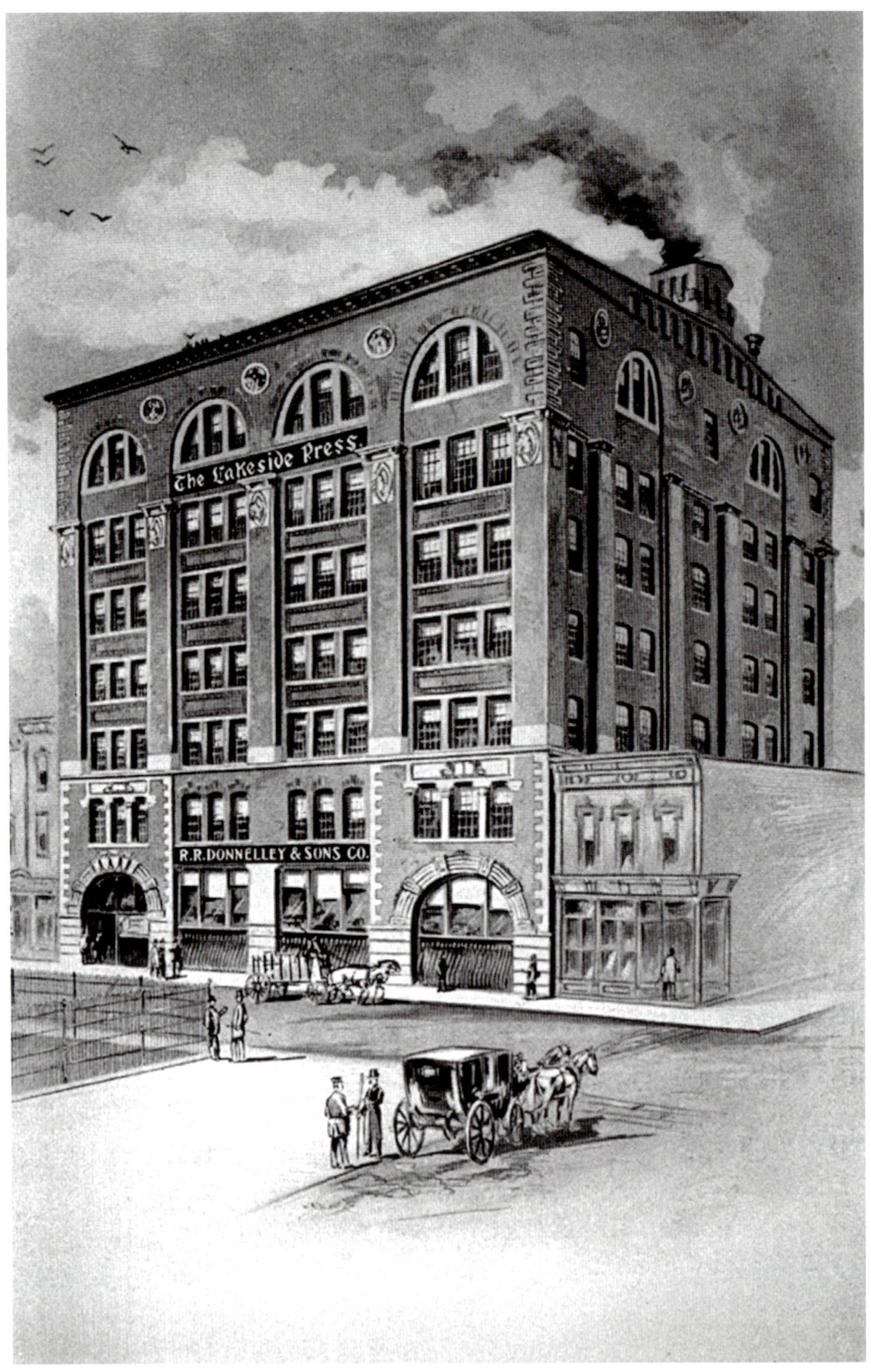

EARLY INDUSTRY: The R. R. Donnelly Press (1864) is one of Chicago's oldest surviving bulk printers. Even though it was an age of horse and wagon, typography methods were improving at full speed and Chicago railroads were rapidly delivering to national clients.

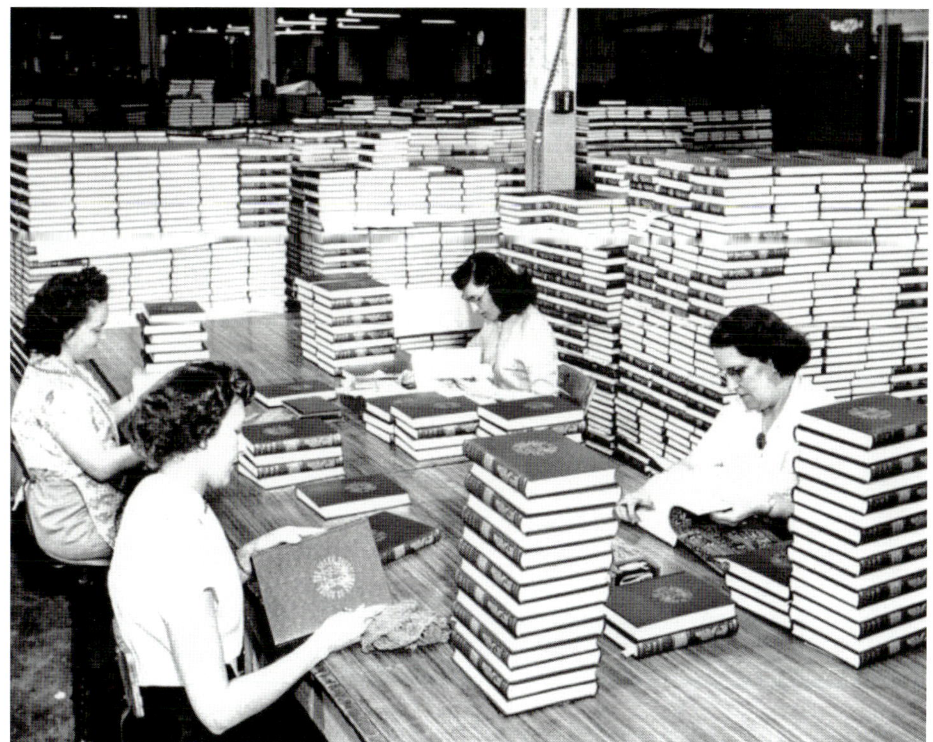

FINE PRINT: Donnelly produced religious books, magazines, telephone directories and school textbooks. Contracts with catalog stores were especially prized among printers since Sears, Wards, and Spiegel were hometown companies that ordered thousands of trade catalogs annually. Today, the old Donnelly building, still stands partly as offices and also as dormitory housing for the many college students in Chicago's South Loop district known as Printer's Row.

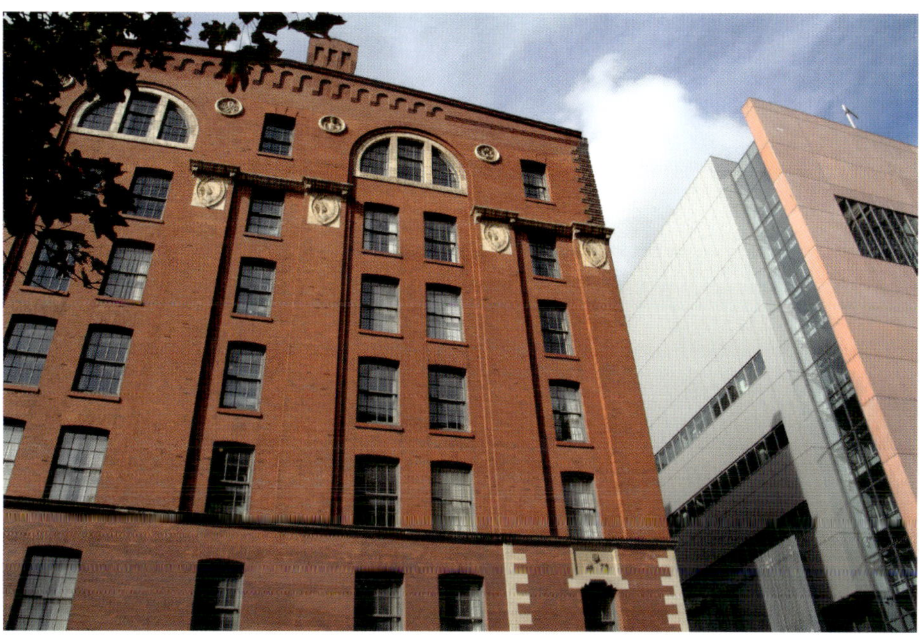

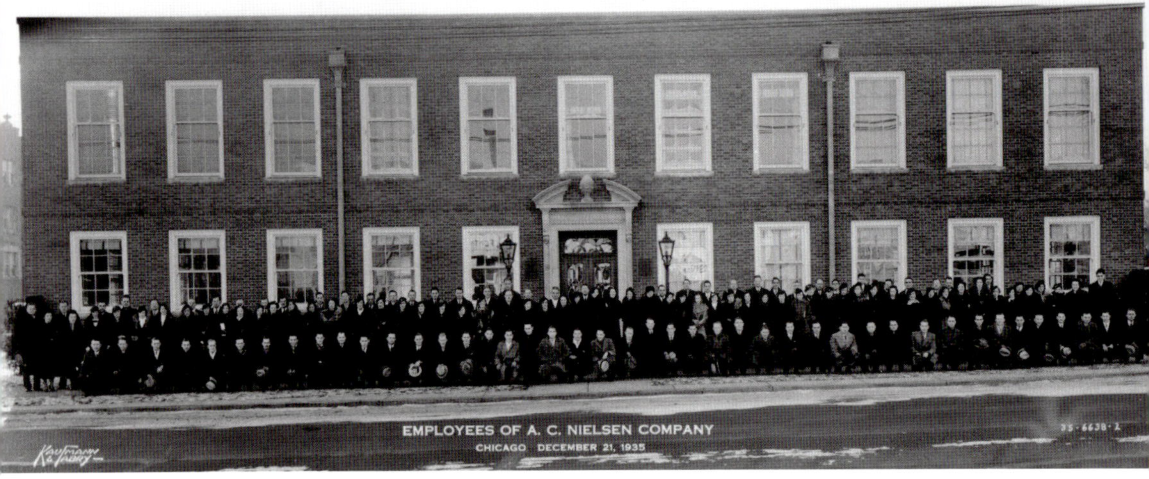

TV RESEARCH: Founded in 1923, the A. C. Nielsen Company was created in the suburb of Skokie, Illinois, for the purpose of collecting data on the effectiveness of television advertising. Nielsen began focusing on several large American cities, but quickly spread services to more than fifty countries beyond the USA. The attached photo shows a Nielsen clerk compiling punch card data from home-based electronic television receivers, an early application of social media analysis in 1956.

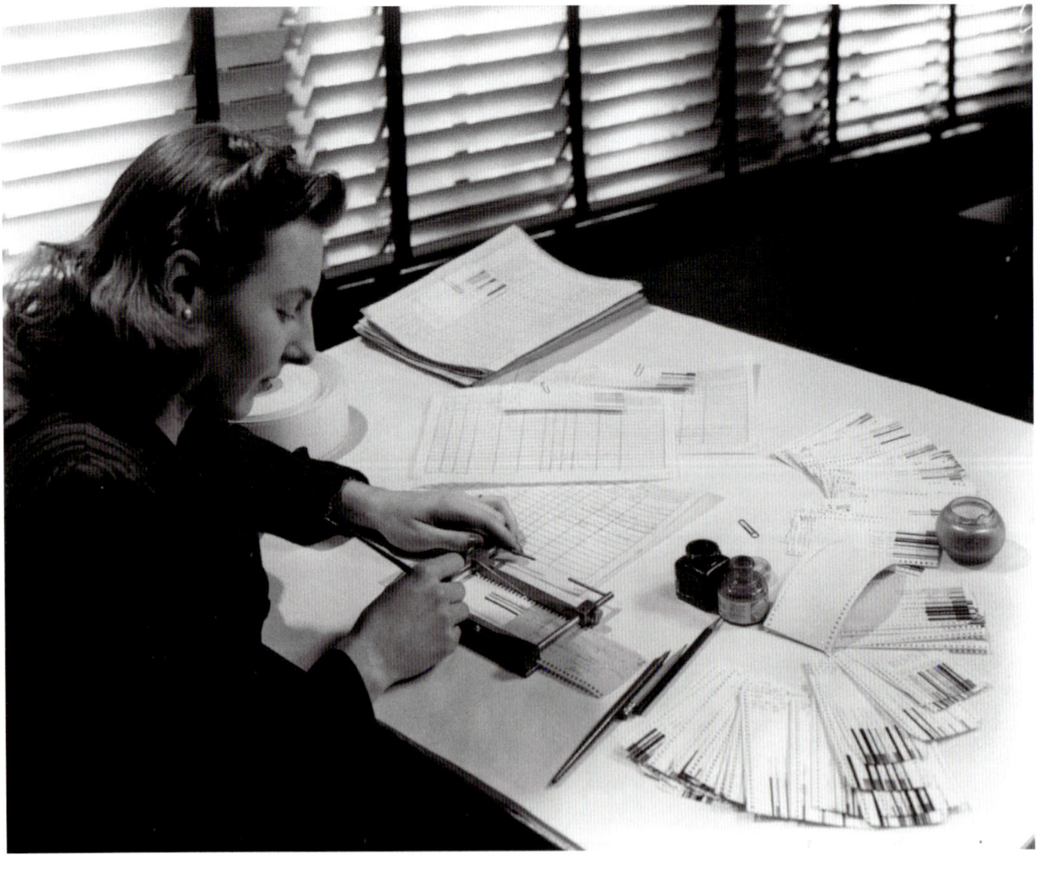

5

RETAILING

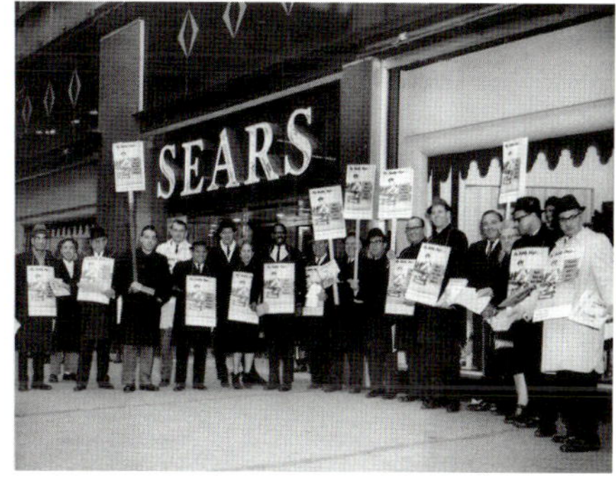

Chicago was the home base for three national retail giants: Montgomery Ward, Sears, and Spiegel Inc. All three offered "catalog operations" across the USA, but all three suffered from financial decline by the 1990s. It is ironic that Wards and Sears pioneered "catalog home shopping," yet got trounced by online shopping a century later.

Two retail giants that did not rely on catalog shopping were Marshall Fields and Carson Pirie Scott. These were luxury stores with high-end reputations, but they mainly served Chicago-area customers. There were smaller retail chains that focused on neighborhood consumers: Wiebolts Inc, Polk Brothers, and Goldblatts stores are examples, but by the 1980s, these companies fell prey to economic overreach. Most Chicago retailers failed to see the enormous competition that regional malls and Big Box stores would offer.

Chicago remains competitive in pharmacy retailing. Walgreen Inc. offered much more than medicine. From 1901, the drugstores competed with national chains like Woolworth's and Kresge's by selling a variety of goods from postcards to fresh milkshakes. Walgreens kept pace with commercial and social trends, and by the 1990s, the drug chain featured drive-up pharmacy windows and in-store clinics. Beyond Chicago, the Walgreen Company today operates in many cities, suburbs, and towns across America.

The trucking industry served a variety of businesses for more than a century. Chicago is an automotive crossroad of America and a hub for many truck lines. Long-haul and intermodal routes cover Illinois and the adjacent states of Wisconsin, Iowa, Kansas, Missouri, and Indiana.

Online shopping trends have been a bonanza for today's trucking industry. Home and store deliveries are made possible through trucking. As in the steel, printing, and food chapters of this book, Chicago retailers relied heavily on the railroad to transport their merchandise. At its peak, Chicago was the terminus for eleven freight railroads. From city to city, railroads are ideal, but for the last few miles, trucks reach the loading dock.

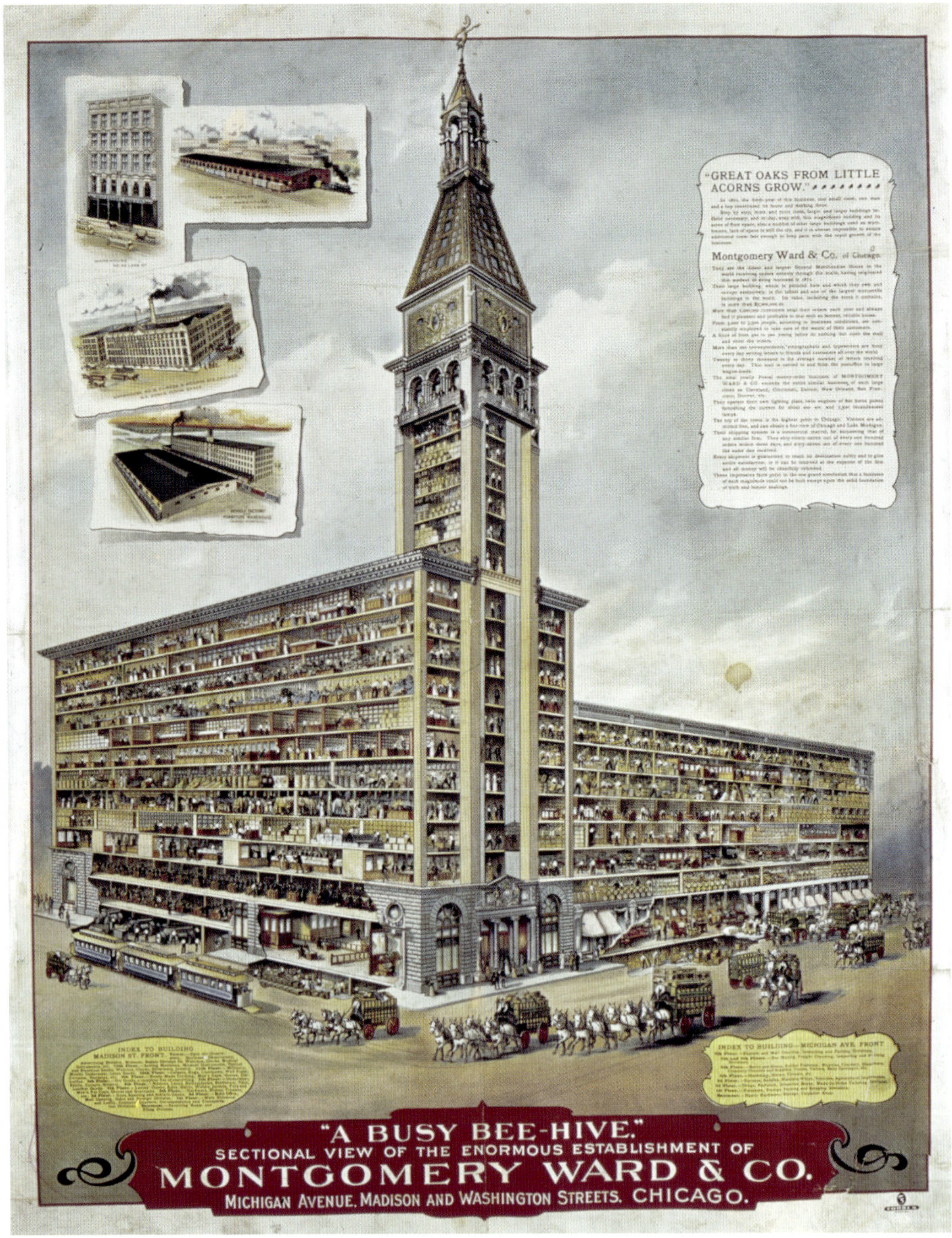

WARD: America's first major mail order operation began in 1872. Stocking, sorting, and mailing merchandise created a "busy beehive" for Montgomery Ward in the heart of downtown Chicago.

SHOP FROM HOME: The Montgomery Ward catalog was the great equalizer. Rural customers were as vital as urban store shoppers. But eventually, the company favored on-street shopping and, by 1941, Wards offered more street outlets than catalog centers. In essence, they abandoned the home-shopping formula that resembled online shopping today. The Ward enterprise ended as the result of owning too many store outlets, too little home-shopping, and too few customers. One retail analyst summarized Ward's economic problem as "too little, too late."

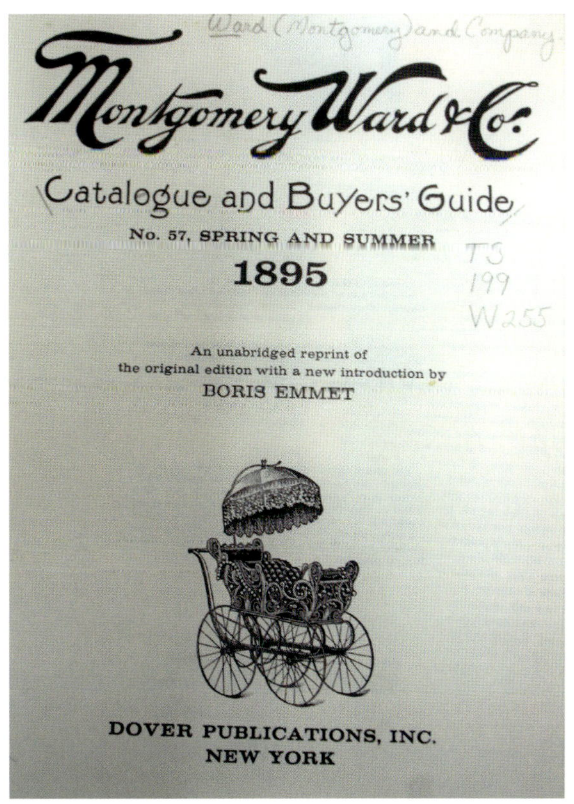

Montgomery Ward & Co.

Catalogue and Buyers' Guide

No. 57, SPRING AND SUMMER

1895

An unabridged reprint of
the original edition with a new introduction by
BORIS EMMET

DOVER PUBLICATIONS, INC.
NEW YORK

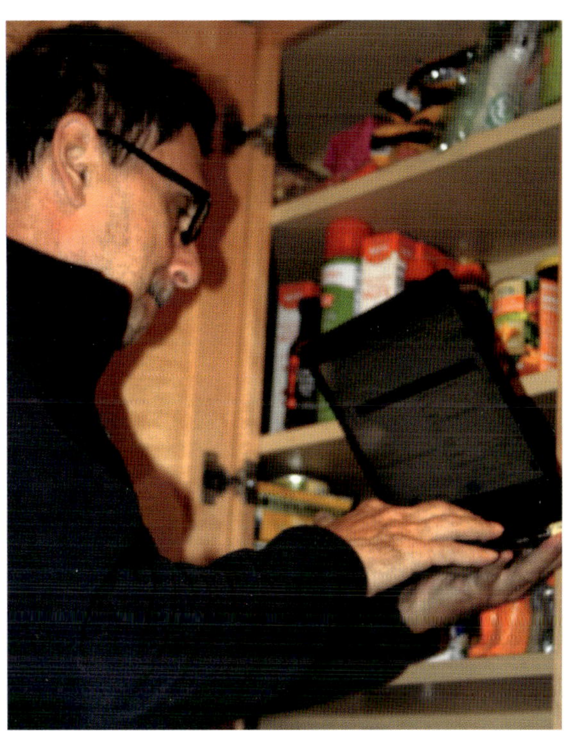

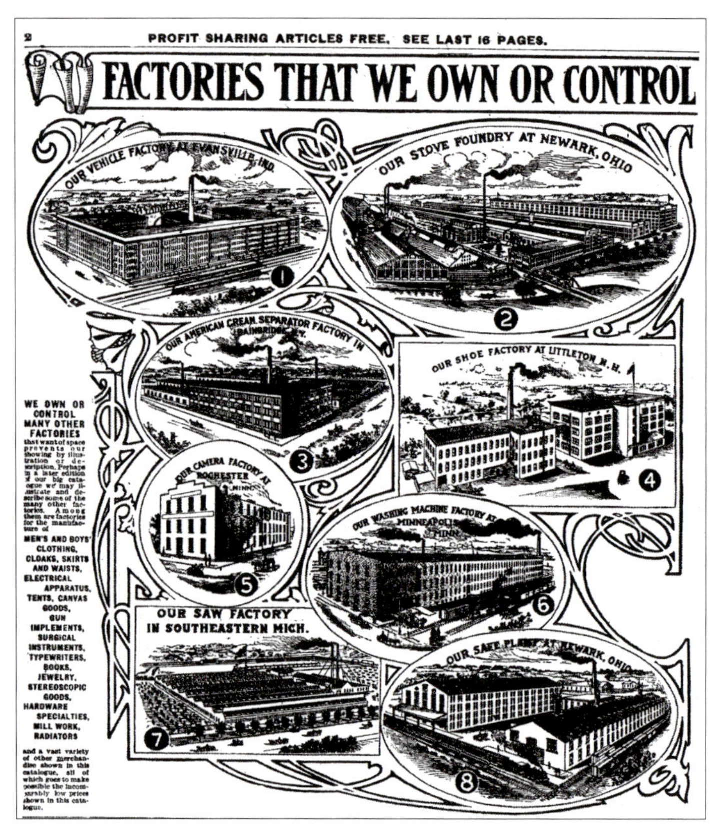

2 PROFIT SHARING ARTICLES FREE. SEE LAST 16 PAGES.

FACTORIES THAT WE OWN OR CONTROL

1. OUR VEHICLE FACTORY AT EVANSVILLE, IND.
2. OUR STOVE FOUNDRY AT NEWARK, OHIO
3. OUR AMERICAN CREAM SEPARATOR FACTORY IN BAINBRIDGE, N.Y.
4. OUR SHOE FACTORY AT LITTLETON, N.H.
5. OUR CAMERA FACTORY AT ROCHESTER, MINN.
6. OUR WASHING MACHINE FACTORY AT MINNEAPOLIS, MINN.
7. OUR SAW FACTORY IN SOUTHEASTERN MICH.
8. OUR SAFE PLANT AT NEWARK, OHIO

WE OWN OR CONTROL MANY OTHER FACTORIES that want of space prevents our showing by illustration or description. Perhaps in a later edition of our big catalogue we may illustrate and describe some of the many other factories. Among them are factories for the manufacture of MEN'S AND BOYS' CLOTHING, CLOAKS, SKIRTS AND WAISTS, ELECTRICAL APPARATUS, TENTS, CANVAS GOODS, GUN IMPLEMENTS, SURGICAL INSTRUMENTS, TYPEWRITERS, BOOKS, JEWELRY, STEREOSCOPIC GOODS, HARDWARE SPECIALTIES, MILL WORK, RADIATORS and a vast variety of other merchandise shown in this catalogue, all of which goes to make possible the incomparably low prices shown in this catalogue.

SEARS: Sears Inc. controlled vast supply chains and used these factories to cut costs. Sears attempted to be both manufacturer and retailer of merchandise. In modern times, factory and store operations are separated by government anti-trust rules. Sears and Montgomery Ward competed for the catalog trade. In 1895, a full Victorian outfit sold on this catalog page for less than $5 dollars—a bargain in the Gilded Age.

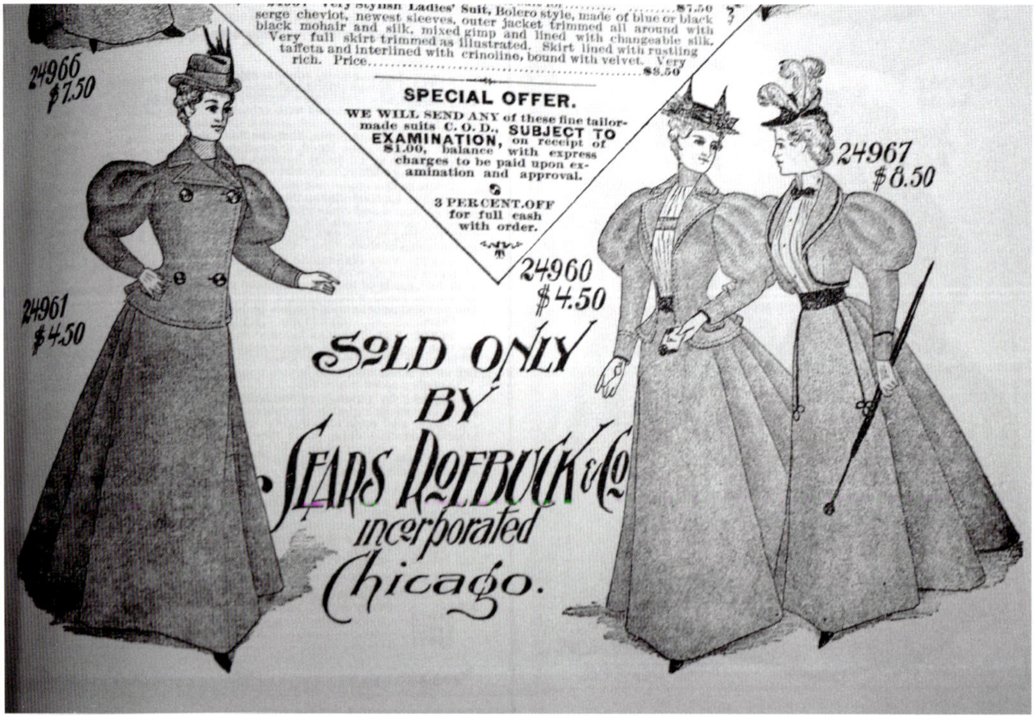

serge cheviot, newest sleeves, outer jacket trimmed all around with black mohair and silk, mixed gimp and lined with changeable silk. Very full skirt trimmed as illustrated. Skirt lined with rustling taffeta and interlined with crinoline, bound with velvet. Very rich. Price..$8.50

SPECIAL OFFER.

WE WILL SEND ANY of these fine tailor-made suits C.O.D., SUBJECT TO EXAMINATION, on receipt of $1.00, balance with express charges to be paid upon examination and approval.

3 PER CENT. OFF for full cash with order.

24966 $7.50

24961 $4.50

24960 $4.50

24967 $8.50

SOLD ONLY BY SEARS ROEBUCK & CO. incorporated Chicago.

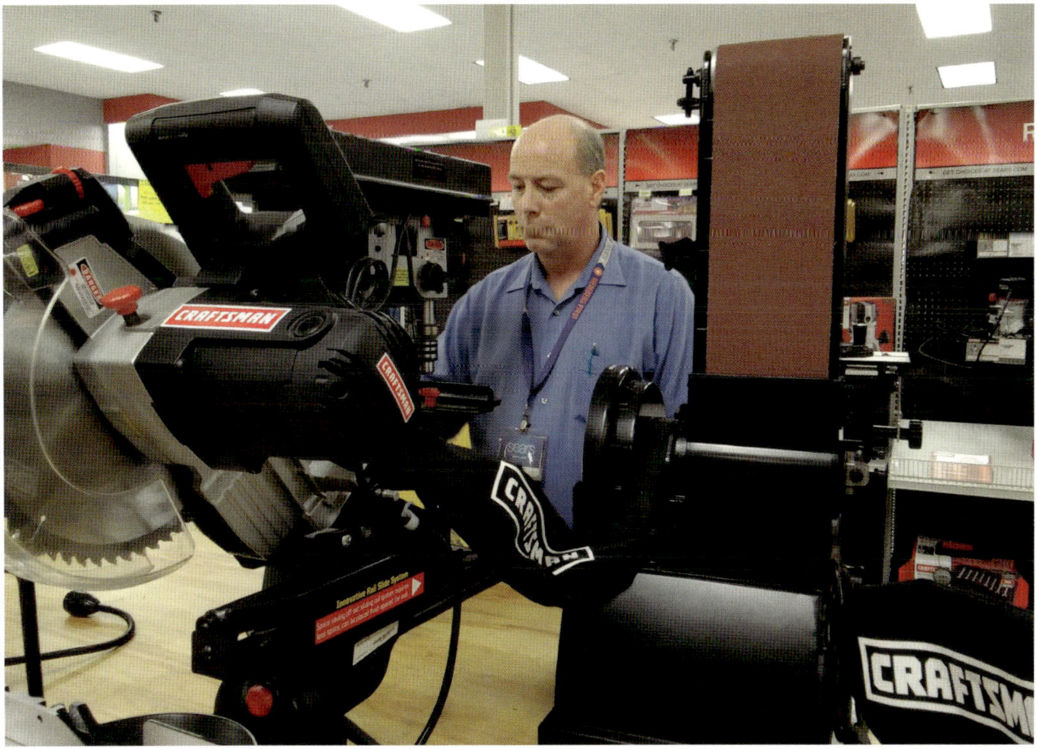

END OF AN ERA: Sears developed durable product lines like Craftsman tools, Kenmore appliances, and even automobile insurance plans. Despite its aggressive retail experience, Sears could not avoid financial collapse. By the year 2000, the flagship stores closed, and all merchandise was sold off through a series of outlet stores.

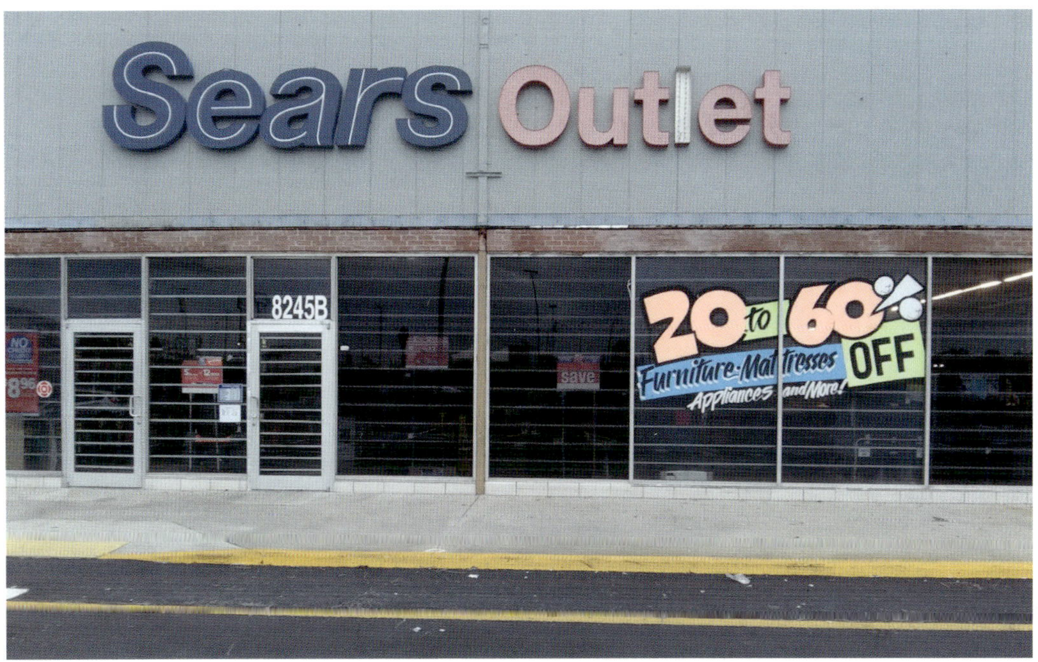

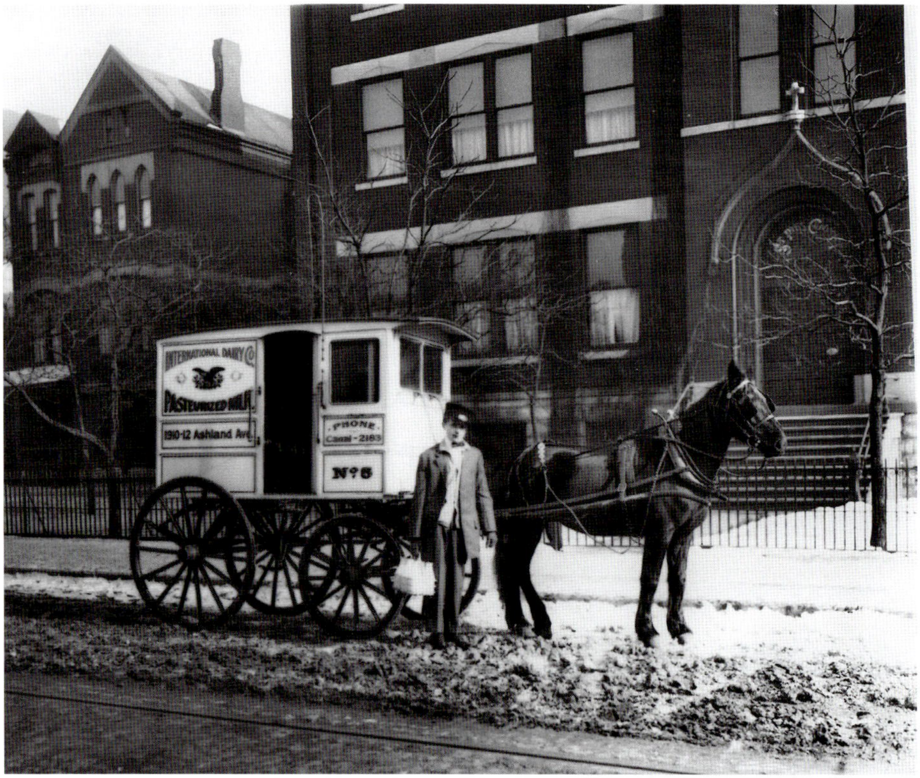

TRUCKING: Operators of horse and wagon were called "teamsters" because they operated teams of mules or horses in harnesses. By the twentieth century, a union of truck drivers called themselves teamsters as well.

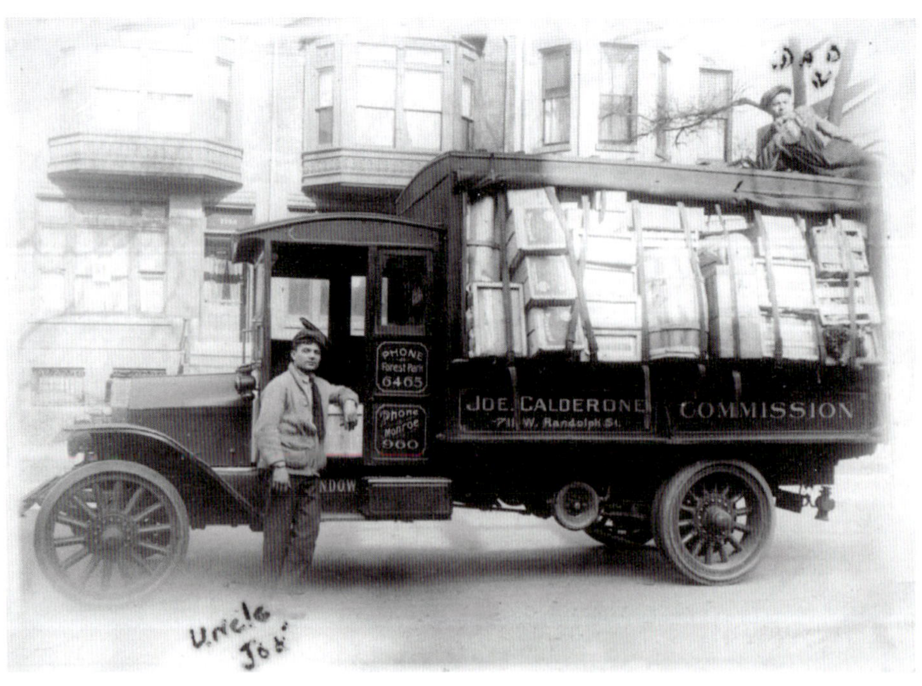

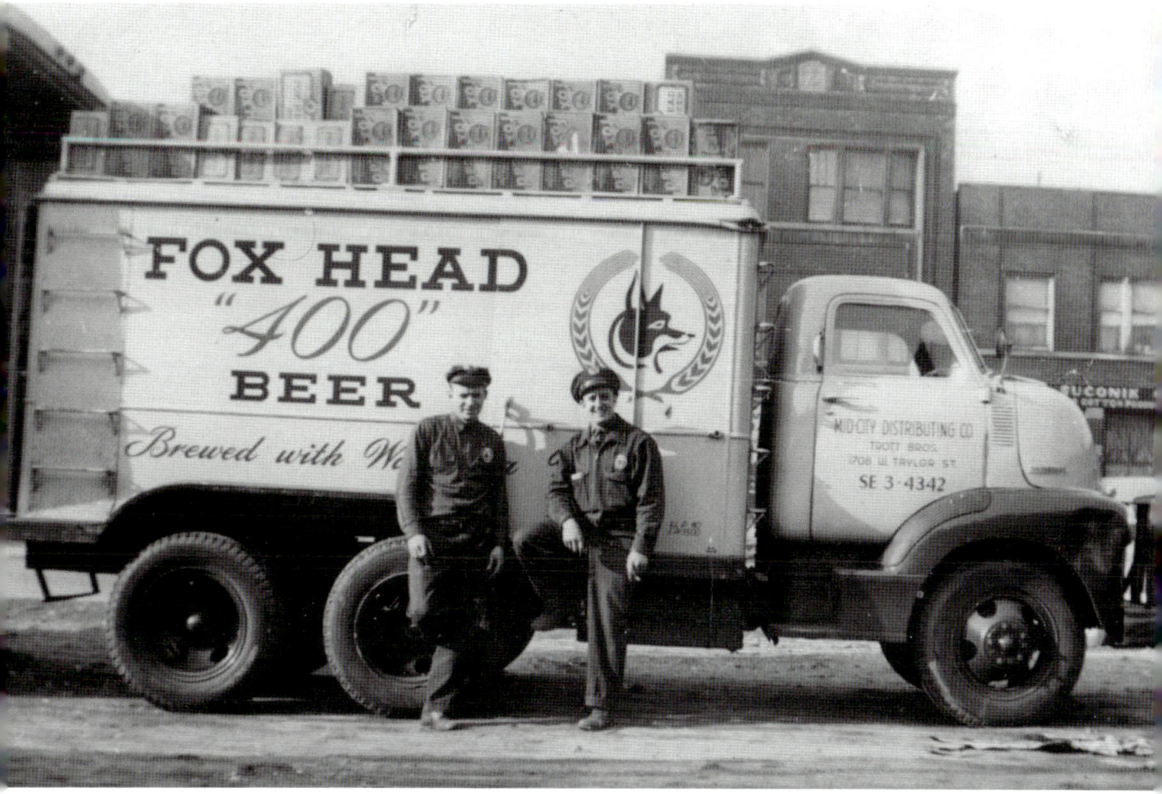

UNION BROTHERS: During the 1950s, the International Teamsters Union recruited thousands of truckers to join the union. After two decades of argument and struggle, most drivers for big manufacturers were unionized. Online shopping and Amazon-type delivery services have caused long-haul drivers and short-haul operators to thrive.

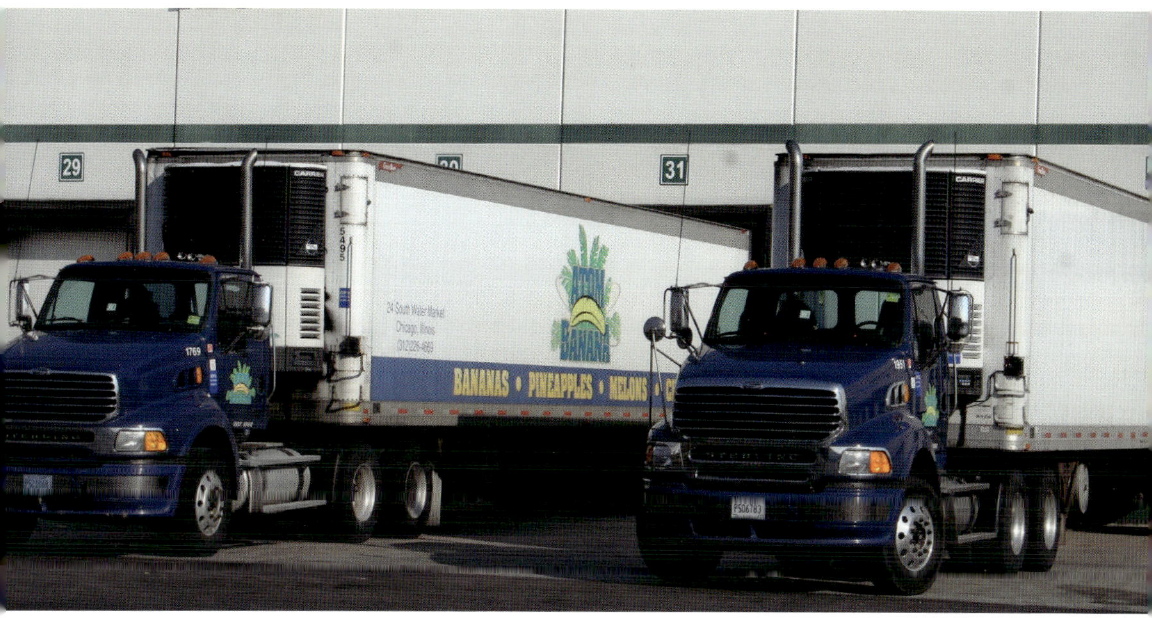

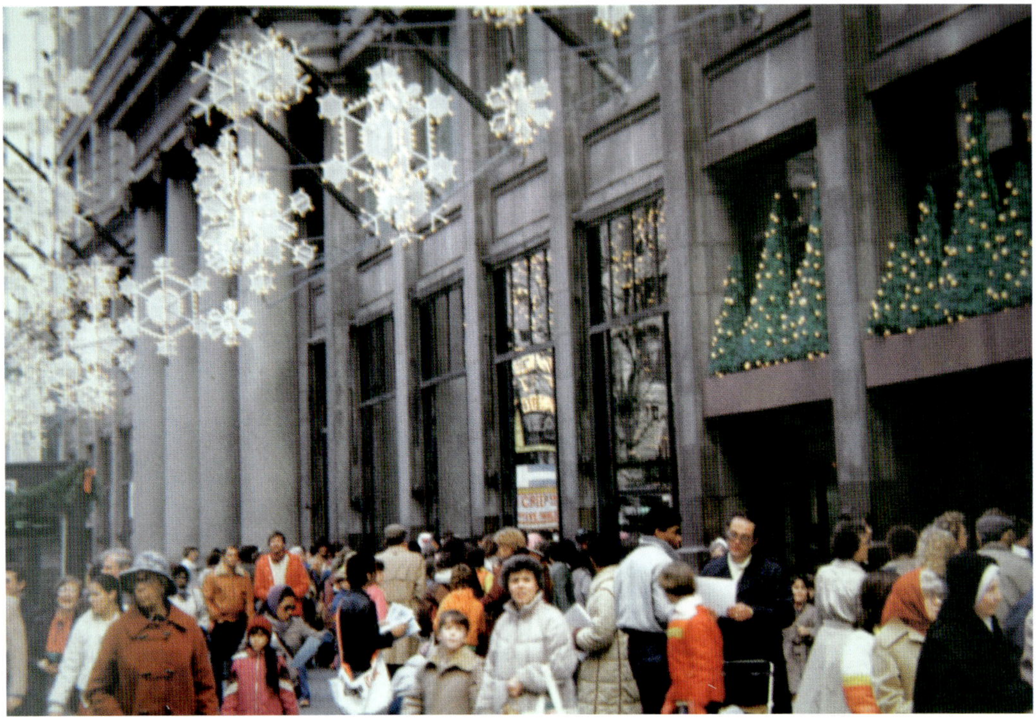

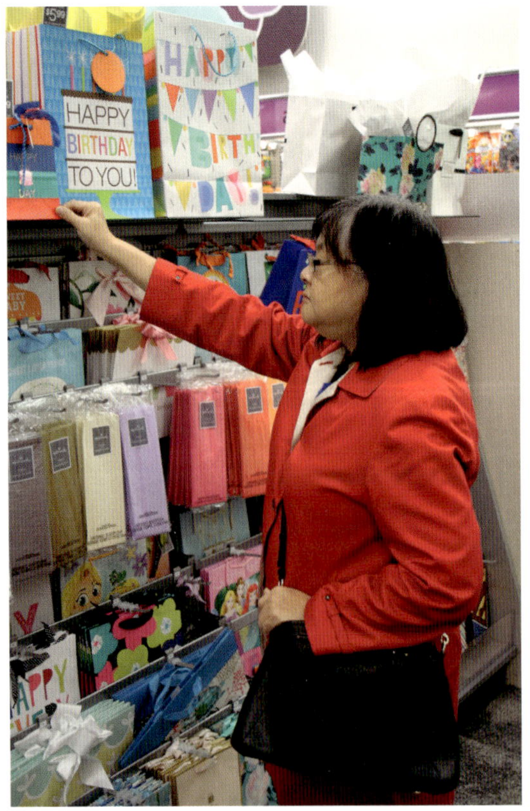

FIELDS AFAR: In 1887, Mr. Marshall Field opened his State Street, Chicago, department store. He retained award-winning architect, Daniel Burnham, to help construct the flagship stores. It was filled with nine floors of "wholesale dry goods"—a palace of luxury merchandise. Today, in an era of high competition, customers expect quality merchandise at wholesale prices. In many ways, Chicago has returned to a frontier of retail choices.

6

Music

For more than 100 years, Chicago has been making music—musical instruments that is. The Lyon & Healy company started in 1864 and is one of the largest continuously operating companies in Chicago. The company still produces harps for symphony orchestras.

The Kimball Company and the Hamilton Corporation were national leaders in piano manufacturing. Hamilton left Chicago Heights in the 1970s. Kimball made its first pianos in 1857 but moved the company to Indiana in 1950.

The Hammond Corporation has been making organs in Chicago since 1938. The Ludwig Drum Company has been producing percussion instruments since 1909 but moved out of state in the 1950s.

Musical instrument manufacturing is an exacting and costly business in America. Many makers are subject to mergers, sell-offs, and buyouts in a tumultuous business environment. Using the Ludwig Drum Company again as an example, the firm has been purchased five times by competitors.

In the realm of recorded music, jukebox manufacturing in Chicago was a short but profitable business. The J. P. Seeburg Company, on Chicago's Northside, was a leader in producing coin-operated machines. Family run during the 1950s, Seeburg filled diners and drive-in cafes with recorded music. The company also experimented with rolled paper music and electronic drums.

The Rock-Ola Corporation, created in 1927, was known for producing parking meters, weighing scales, and furniture cabinets. But bigger profits were made in manufacturing jukeboxes. By the 1980s, Rock-Ola created coin-operated video games that were profitable.

In the realm of music production, the Chess Brothers Recording Studio is legendary. During the 1950s to 1960s, Blues artists such as Muddy Waters, Howlin' Wolf, Koko Taylor, and Willie Dixon cut 45 and 33 RPM records at Chess. Today, the Willie Dixon Blues Heaven Foundation occupies the original Chess recording studio at 2120 S. Michigan Avenue. The foundation provides public tours and memorabilia from the Blues Era.

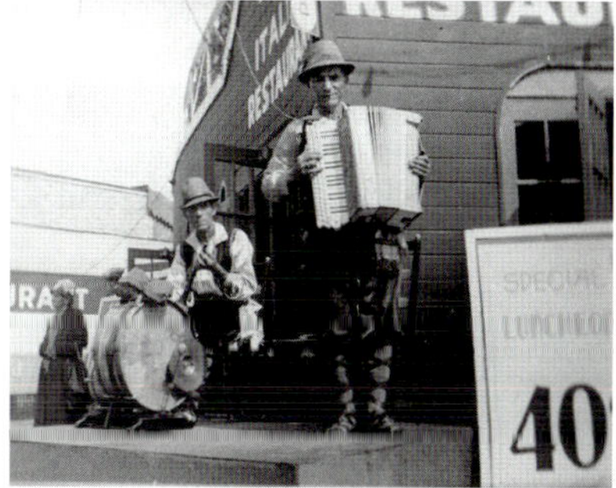

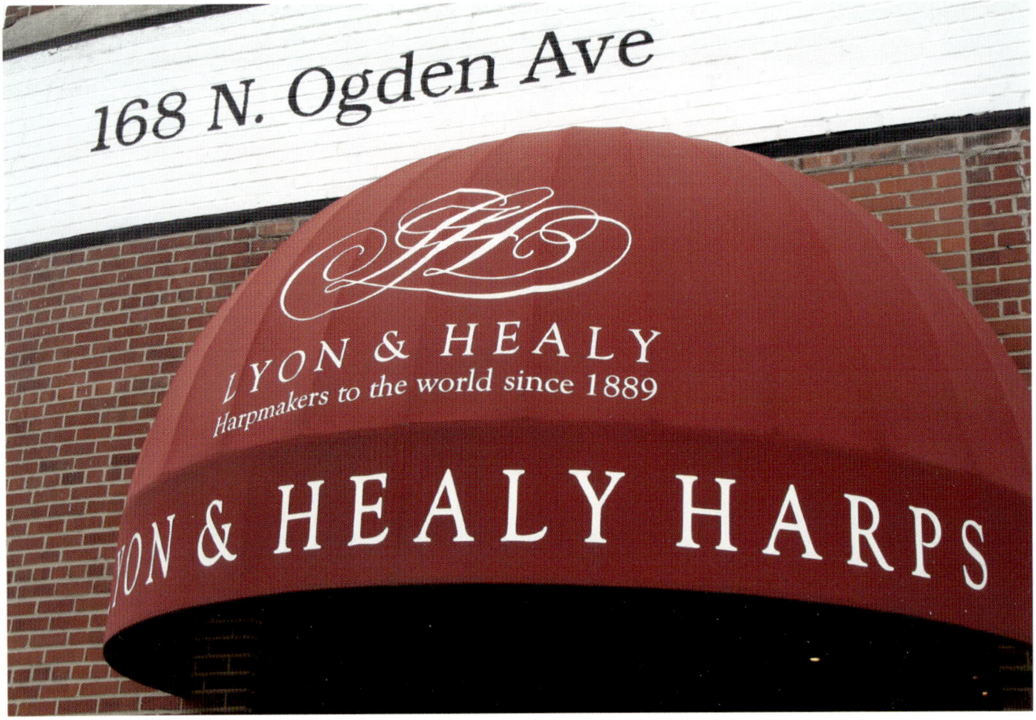

STRINGS ATTACHED: Lyon and Healy Company is the oldest producer of musical harps in America. More instruments produced by the company include drums, guitars, and pianos. The factory, located on Chicago's Westside, was established in 1889, making this one of the oldest continuous music manufacturers in town. Brass bands were ideal for marching and dancing. Before radio was invented, live dance bands were popular, too.

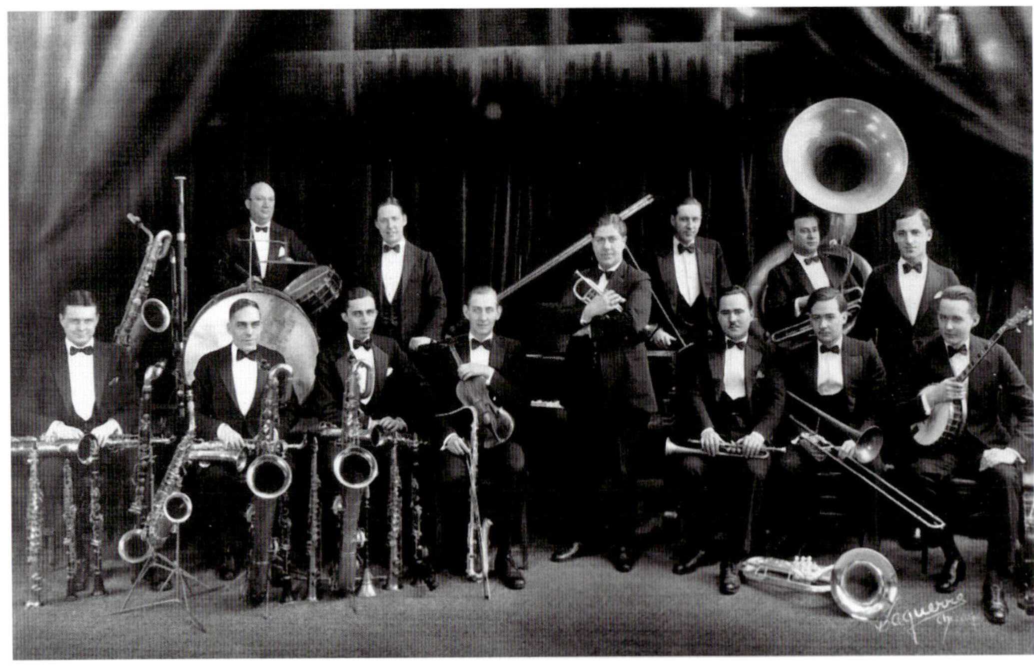

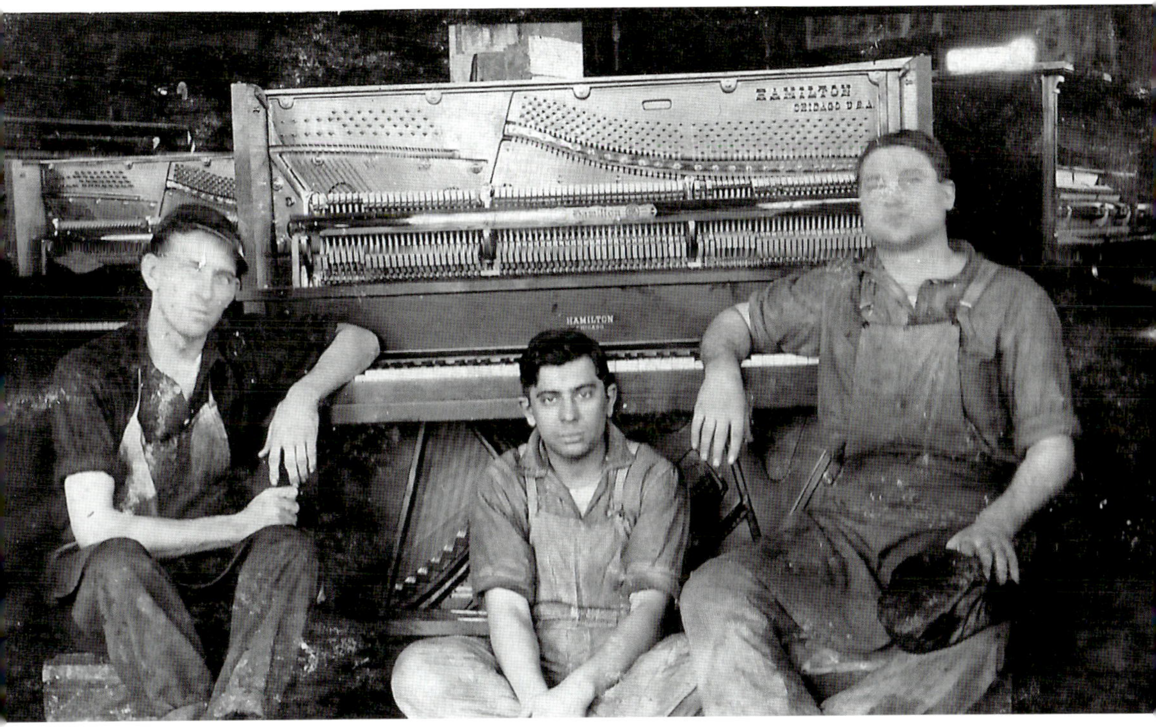

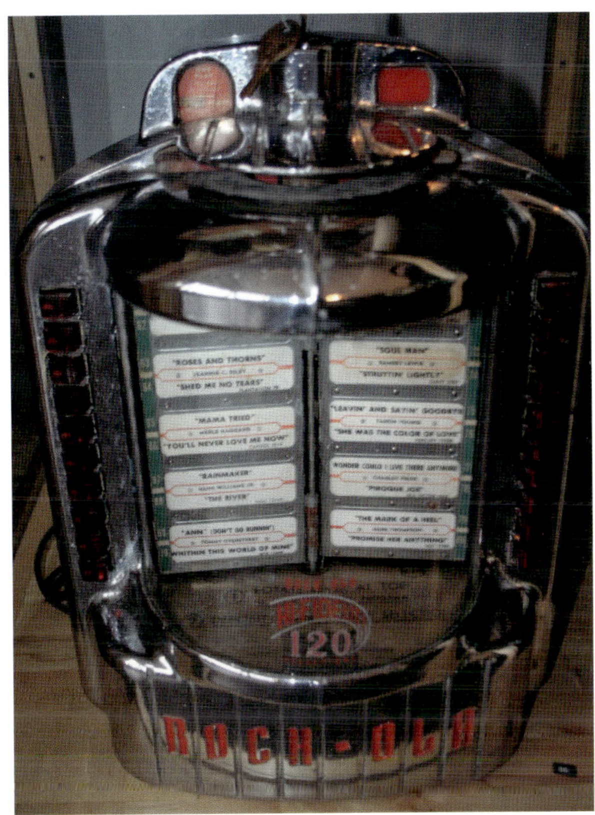

Music Rivals: The Hamilton Piano Company was a busy employer in Chicago Heights. Hamilton produced upright pianos while the Kimball Company was the city rival for expensive symphonic pianos. The Rock-Ola Company produced elaborate jukeboxes for cafes and taverns in Chicago. These jukeboxes are still in production today, but under another firm.

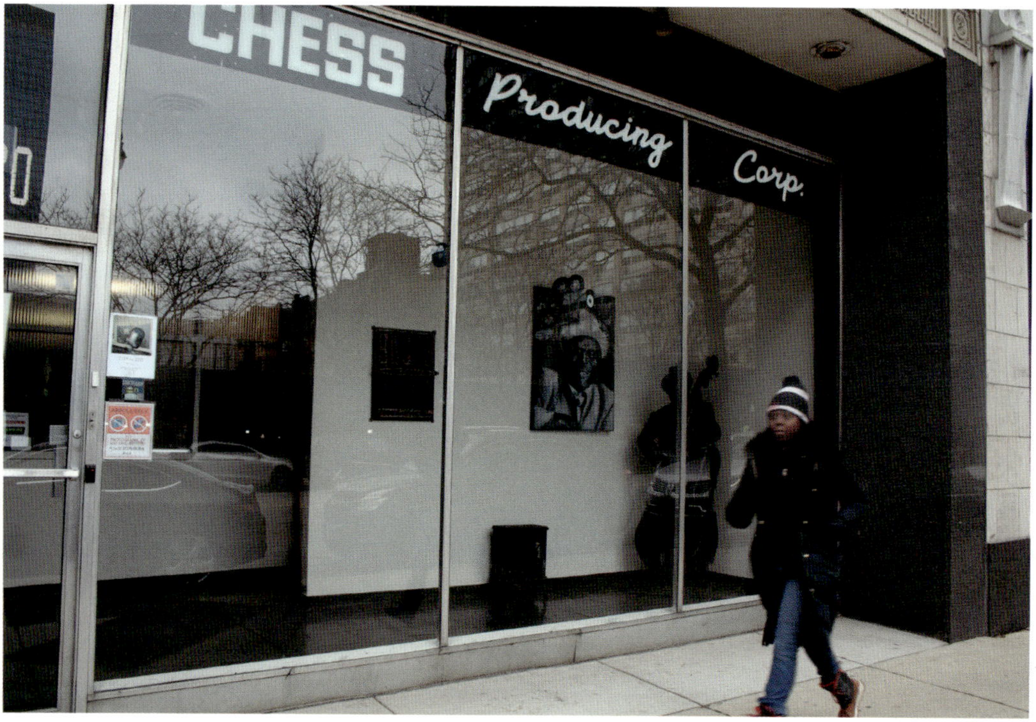

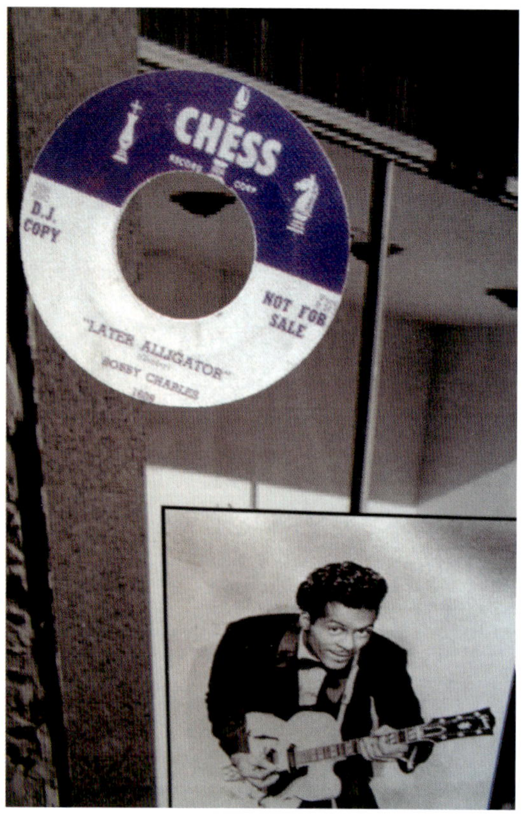

CHESS MATCH: Phil, Leonard and Marshall Chess established Chess Recording Co. in 1950. One of their largest recording studios still stands today at 2120 S. Michigan Avenue and is open to the public as a musical museum. Chess Bros. promotes rhythm & blues, gospel music, soul music, and jazz.

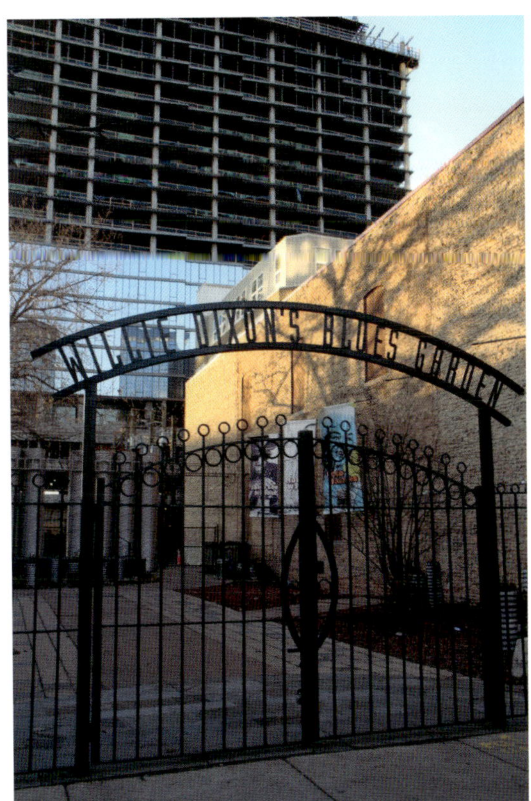

THEN AND NOW: Many well- known artists recorded with Chess Records: Howlin' Wolf, Willie Dixon, Muddy Waters, Chuck Berry, Eric Clapton, and the Rolling Stones are a sampling of musical artists associated with Chess. By 1980, the studios were converted to the Willie Dixon Foundation by his family, who continue to to sustain a museum and famous Blues Garden today.

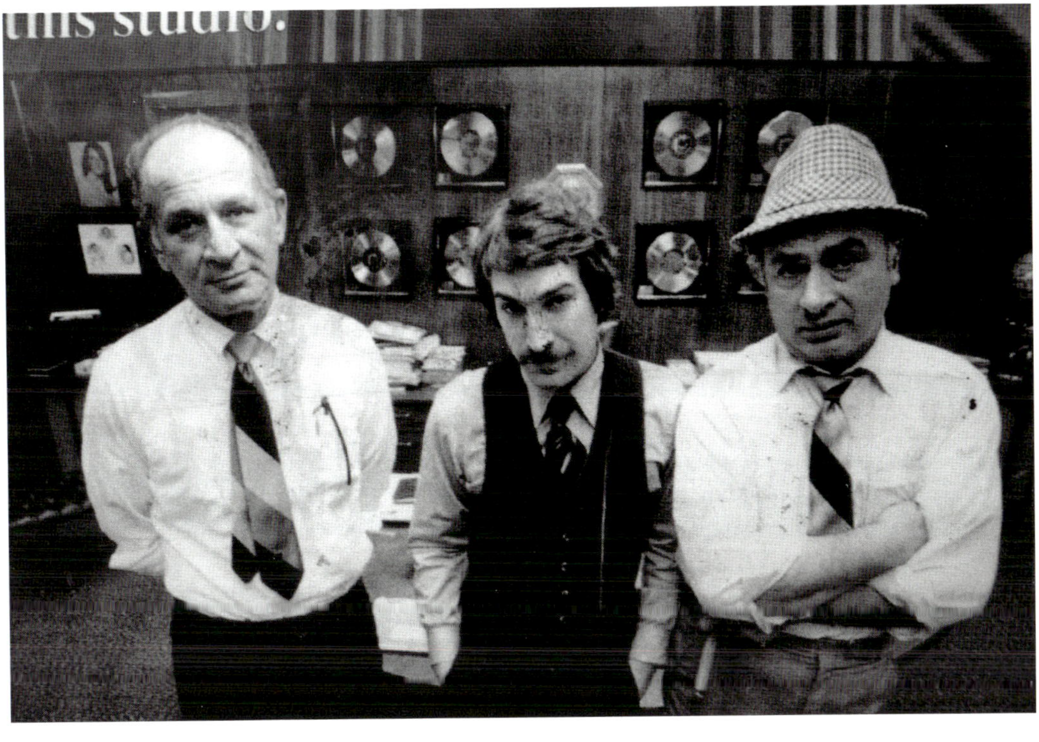

7

CANDY

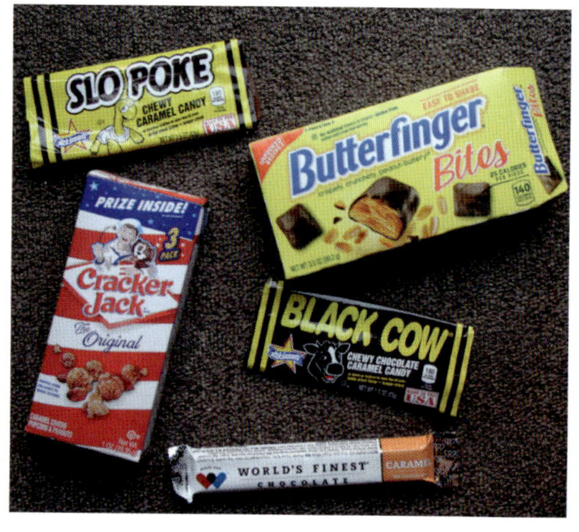

As a national leader in candy production, Chicago manufactures many tons of mass-produced sweet treats: Tootsie Rolls, Double Mint Gum, Whoppers, Slow Pokes, Junior Mints, O'Henry bars, Milk Duds, Juicy Fruit Gum, and Dove Bars.

In his book, *Chicago's Sweet Story*, Leslie Goddard reports that the city's Golden Age of production was during the 1910s to the 1920s, when nearly 100 companies, or one-third of America's candy production, was based in the Chicago area. This was the era of Snickers, Milky Way, Butterfinger, and other popular chocolate treats.

Since 1923, the Mars Company developed a variety of popular candy products such as Twix, M&Ms, Starburst, and Skittles. The popular Three Musketeers candy bar was invented at their European factory, but today, the candy is processed at the Mars, Middle East plant among many other overseas sites.

The Blommer Chocolate Company was another long-time producer in Chicago since 1939. Blommer was not a retailer of wrapped candy. Instead, the company supplied other manufacturers with processed cocoa beans and raw chocolate for refinement. This was a winning formula for Blommer until it sold off the company in 2018 to a Japanese firm.

The William J. Wrigley Company was a leader in Chicago candy production since 1892. Their first product was spearmint flavored gum, but later Wrigley added a variety of gum flavors such as Double Mint, Juicy Fruit, Freedent, and Big Red. By the 1960s, the company also invested in real estate, American League baseball, and other large enterprises.

There are regular industrial tours of the candy making process in Chicago. Visitors can learn how Tootsie Rolls, Lemonheads, and other local candies are created.

GUM CITY: One critic called it a Spanish Gothic Skyscraper; the Wrigley Tower has attracted tourist attention since 1924. The building marks the spot where the Chicago River meets Lake Michigan waters. Wrigley Spearmint Gum is not the company's only brand, but advertising has created a customer stampede. Double Mint, Juicy Fruit, Hubba Bubba, and Freedent are a few brands that have earned millions of customers, too.

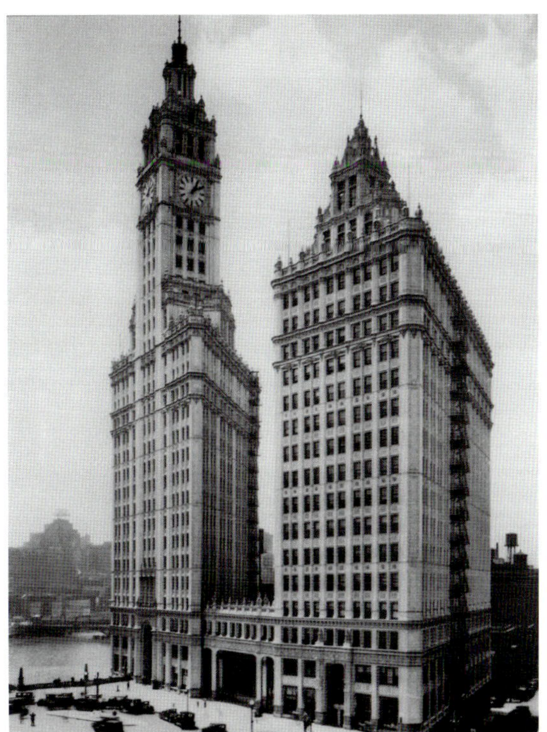

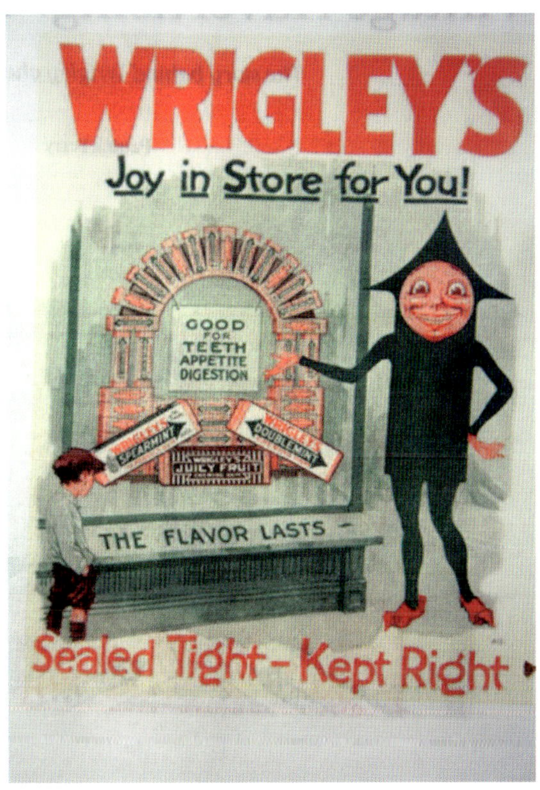

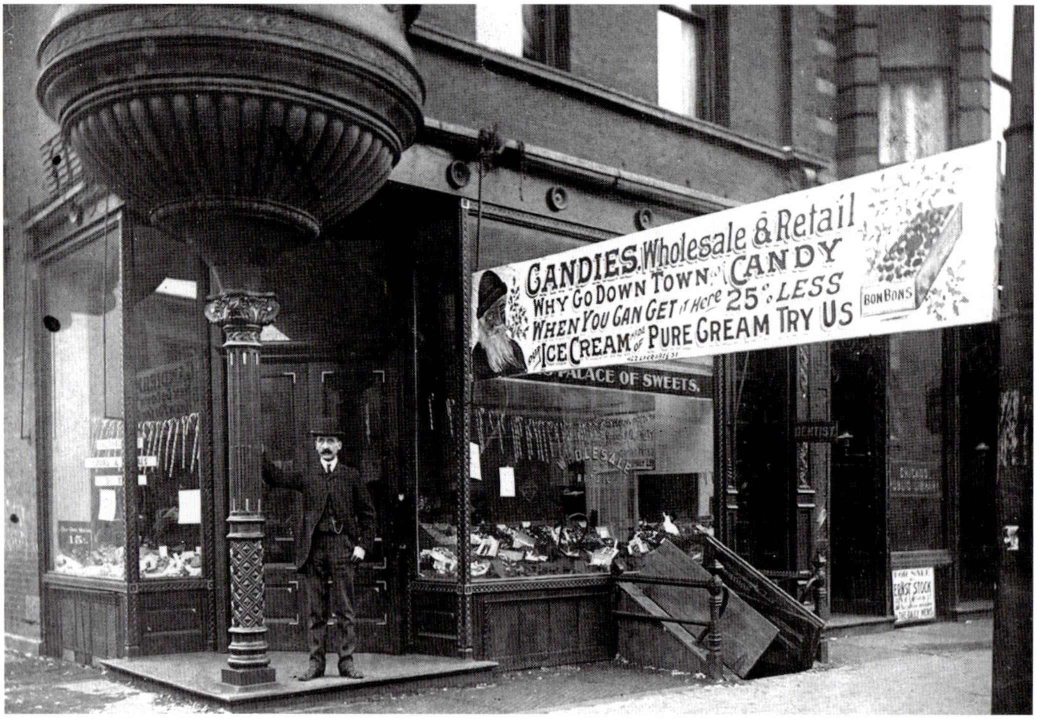

Out of the Kitchen: With a kitchen in the back of the building and customers in the front, Emil Brach and his two sons started a candy shop in 1904. Ten years later the family constructed a full factory with railroad cars to pick up ingredients and deliver the sweets to market.

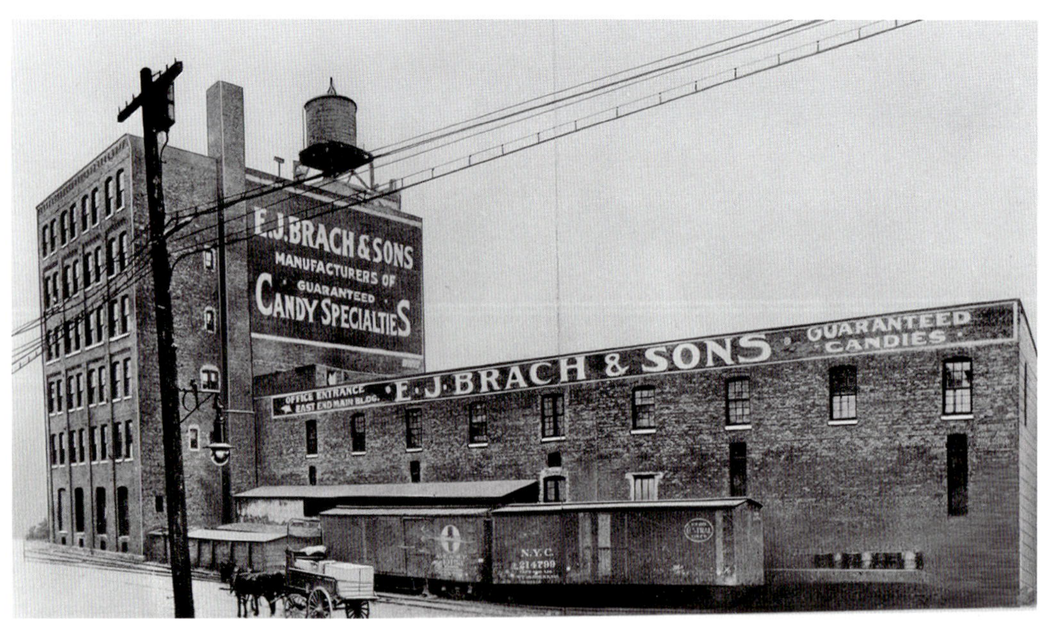

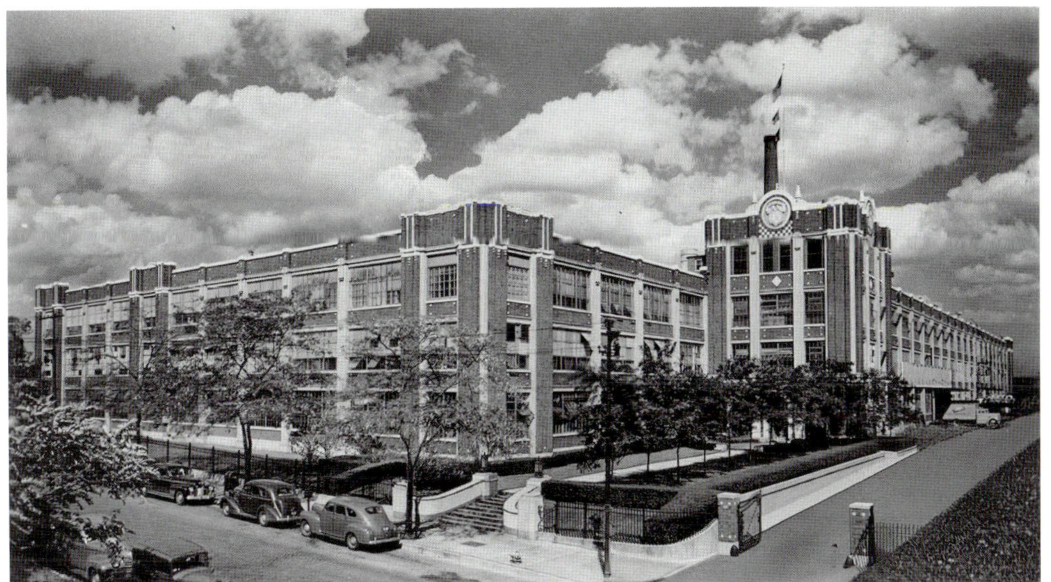

IT'S THE ARCHITECTURE: By 1923, Brach's established an enormous factory on Cicero Avenue, aptly designed by Alfred Alschuler, who was also the architect for the Florsheim and Donnelly factories, mentioned earlier in this book. Today, Brachs candy is found on most supermarket shelves, but the company is now managed by Ferrara Pan Candy Company of Illinois.

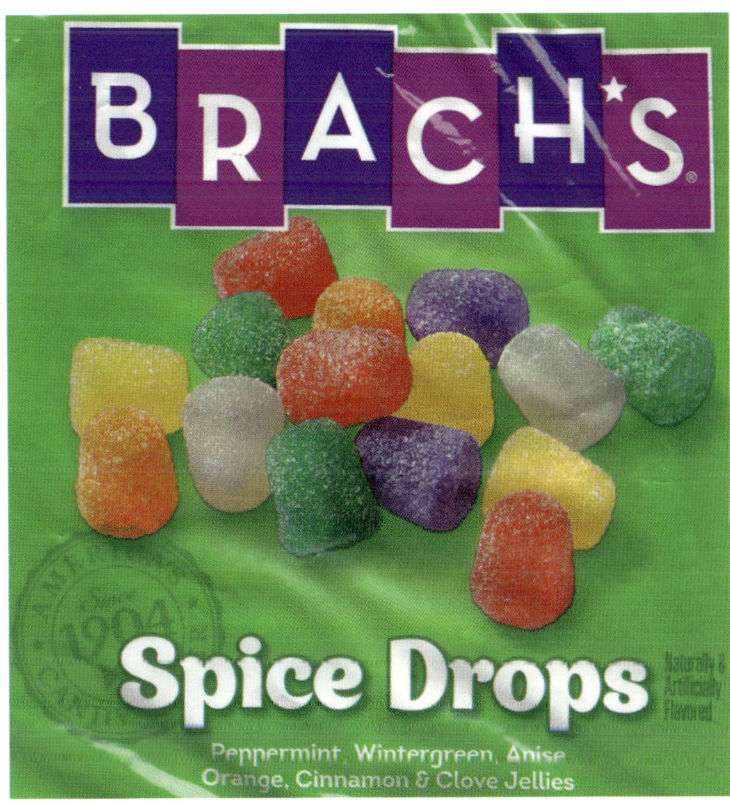

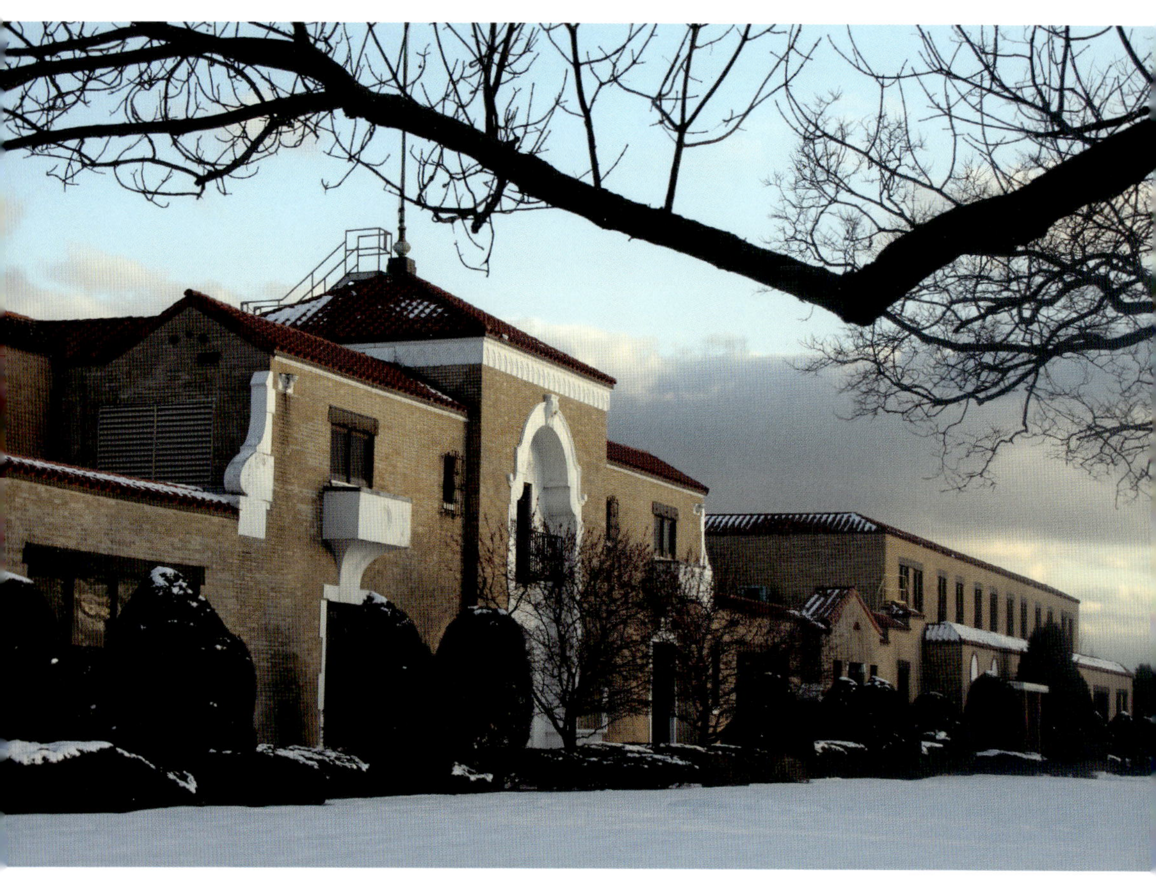

DELUXE MANUFACTURING: This Chicago plant from 1929 is the oldest operating factory in the Mars Candy Corporation network. It resembles a Renaissance-Deco hotel more than a factory. Mars invented Milky Way candy in 1923 and Snickers bars in 1930. Later, the company introduced Starburst, Twix, and Skittles candies. Mars, in more recent years, purchased the recipes for Wrigley Gum and M&M candies. It remains as one of the largest candy makers in the world.

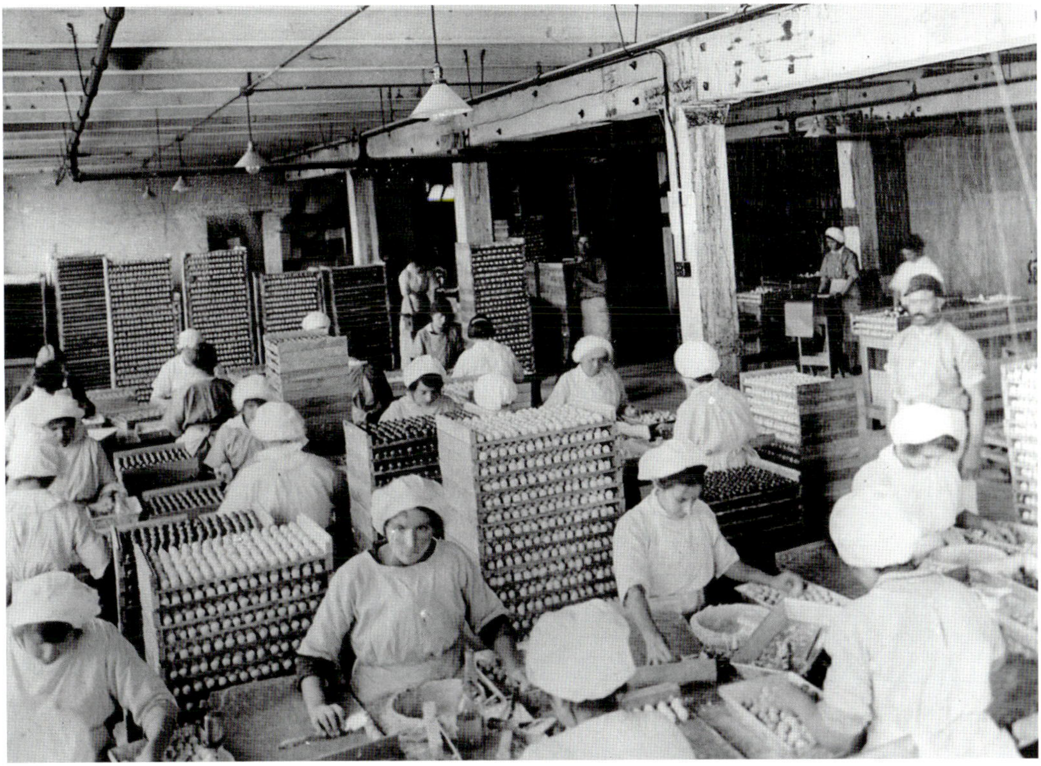

LAYERS OF WORK: The making of Bon Bons was an art form at Mars. This photo in 1919 shows women rolling each piece by hand then applying chocolate coating by machine. Mars invented Milky Way in 1923 and Snickers in 1930. Later the company introduced Starburst, Twix, and Skittles. Mars in more recent years purchased the recipes for Wrigley Gum and M&Ms. Mars continues as one of the largest candy makers in the world

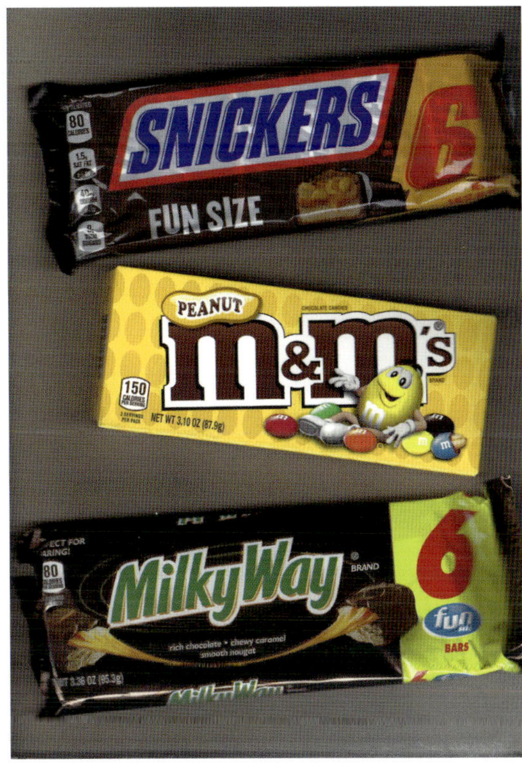

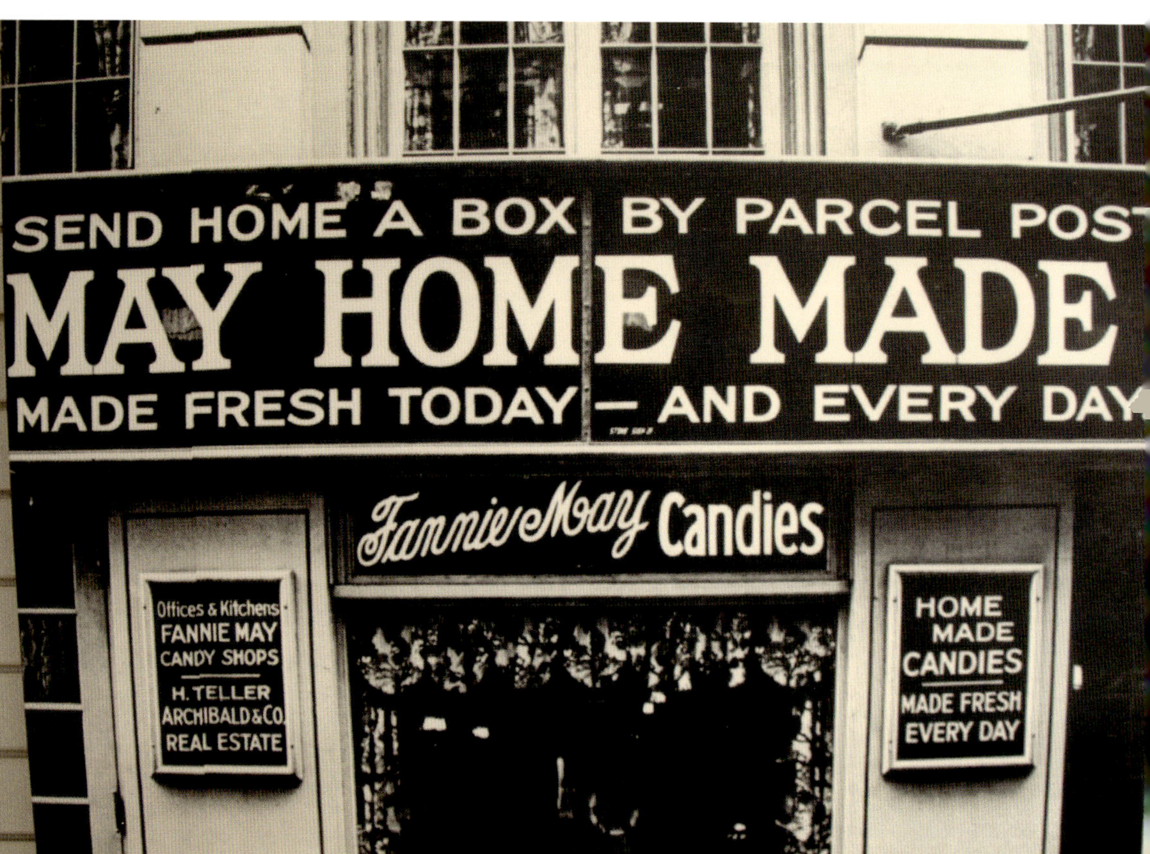

FANNIE MAY: For years, Fannie May has operated in Chicago under several corporate sponsors. It is a traditional downtown landmark store for sweet treats.

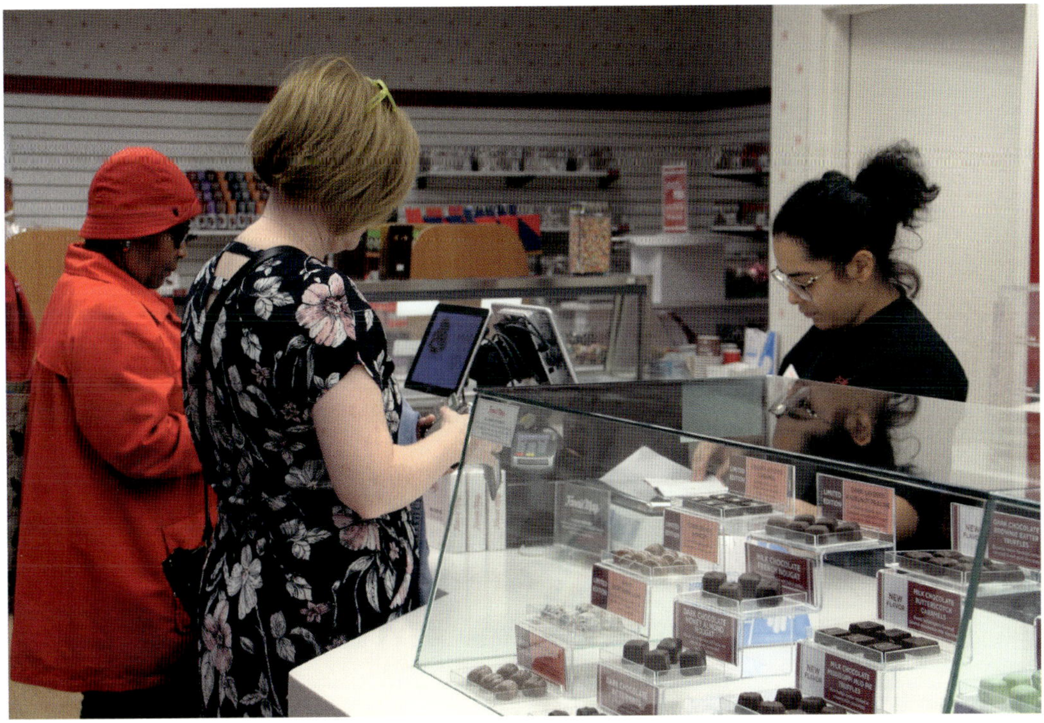

HOME RUNS: The rich mint chocolates and eggnog creams are popular products at Fannie May. Here, shoppers in the Chicago Loop make a "sweet stop" at the Michigan Avenue store. Fannie May is a partnering sponsor of the Chicago Cubs baseball team and sells a line of "Cubs Candy" at Wrigley Field.

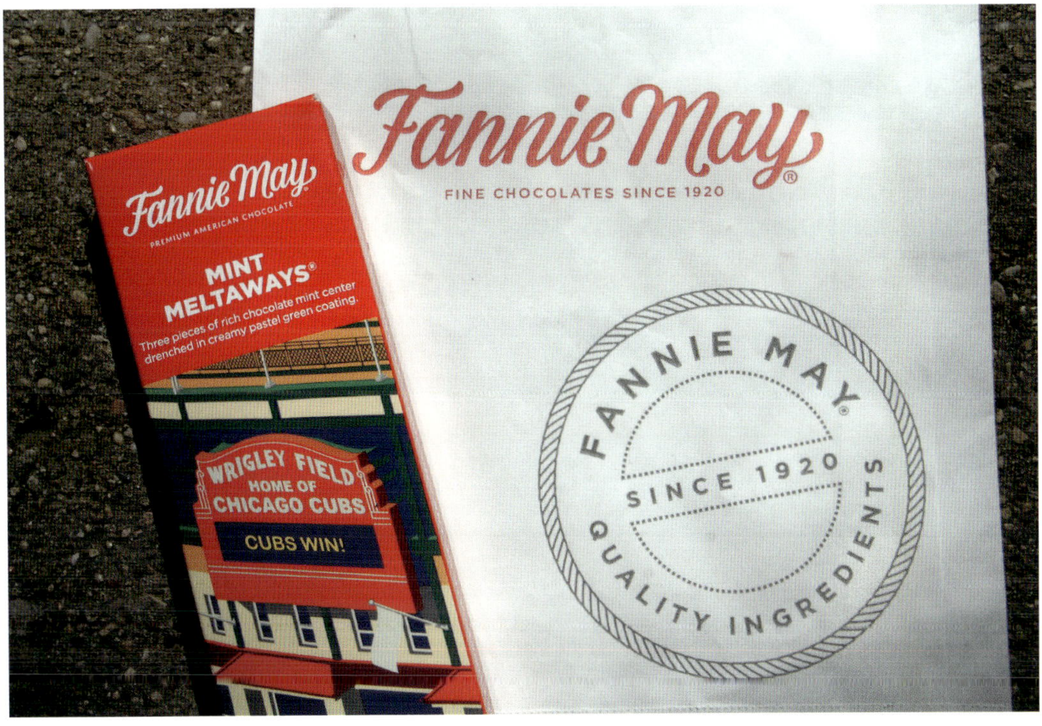

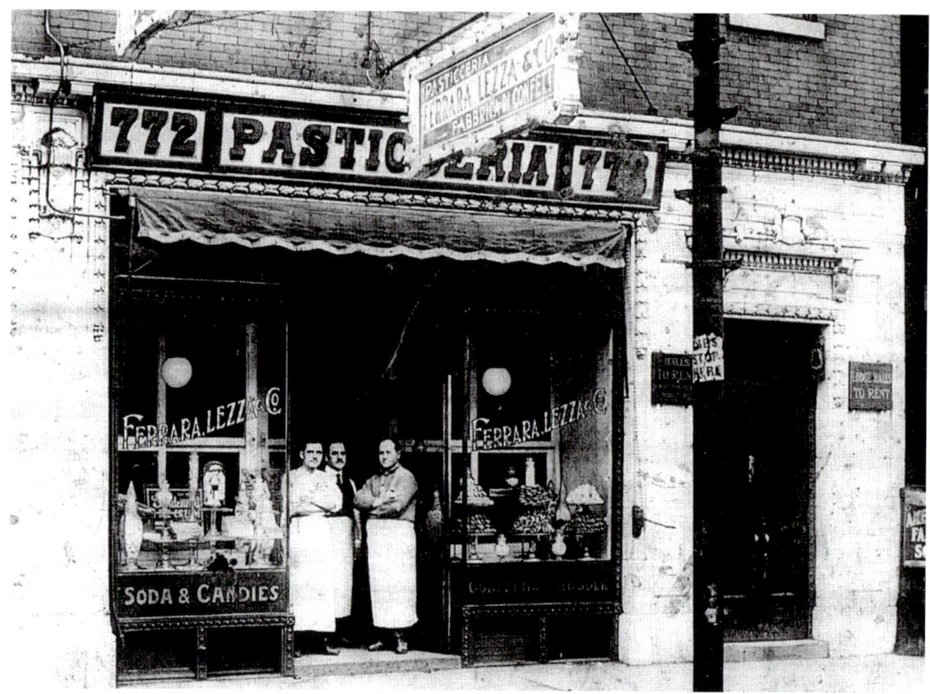

FERRARA TREATS: In 1908, Salvatore Ferrara and his family opened a confectionery shop in Chicago's Little Italy neighborhood. The store made cookies and "confetti" (candy coated almonds) for wedding ceremonies. A branch of the Ferrara family moved to full-scale candy manufacturing in the suburb of Forest Park. Rail transport of raw materials and packaged candy made stops near Harlem Avenue.

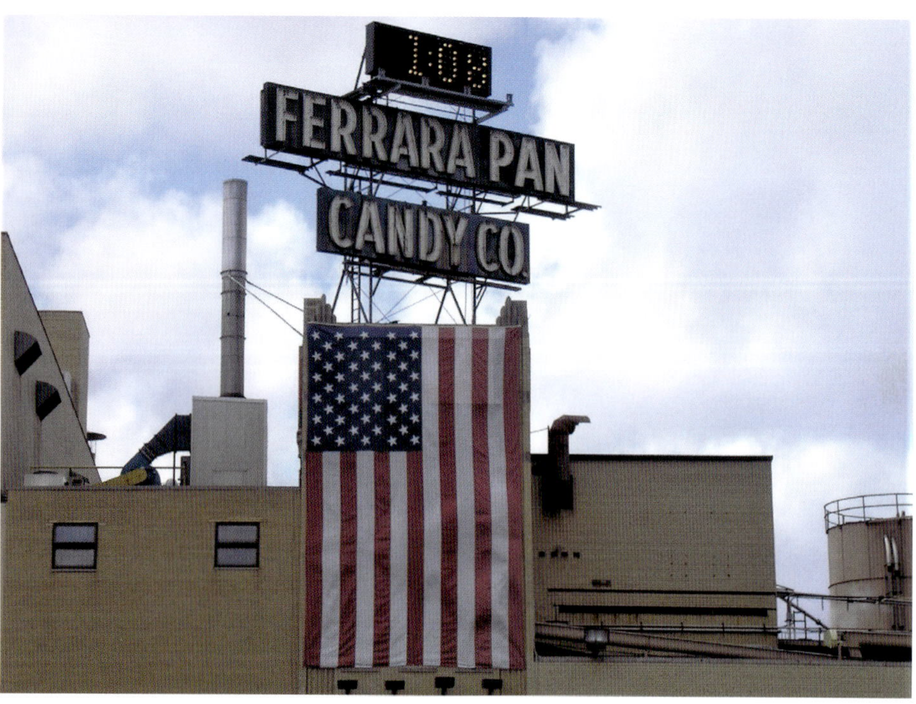

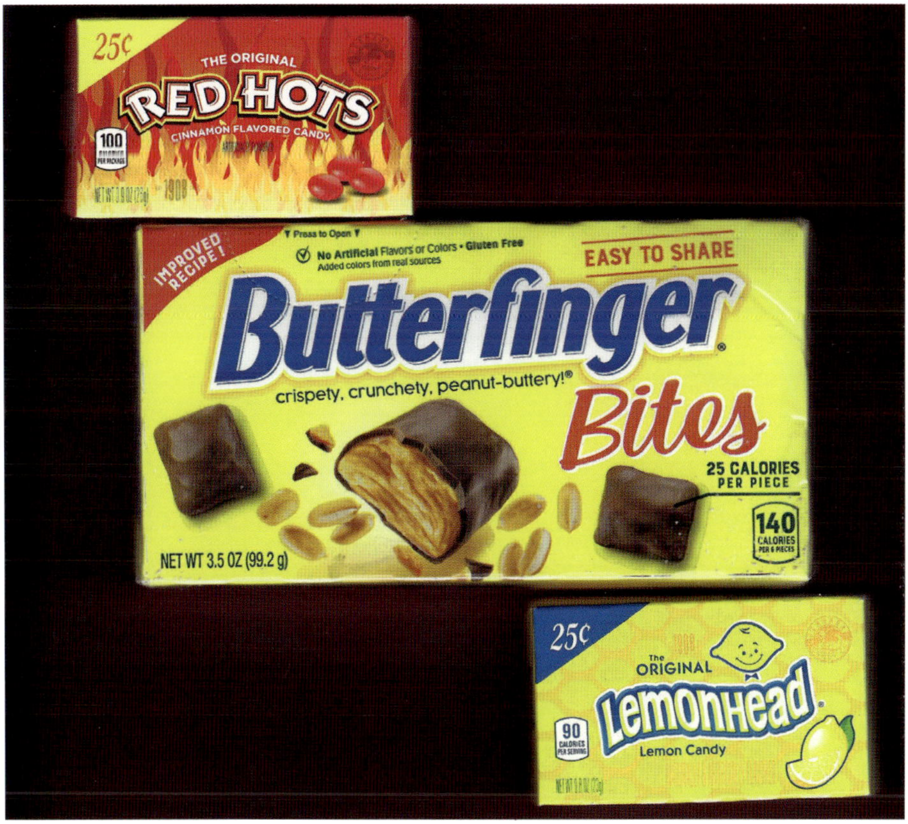

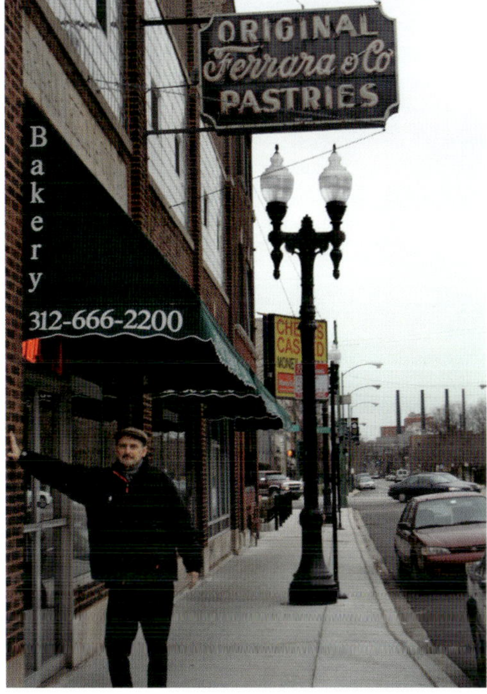

HOT CANDY: Ferrara is still known for producing Red Hots and Fireball brands of candies. The company also handles the famous Butterfinger candy bars once produced solely in Chicago by the Curtis Candy Company. Today, the original Ferrara bakery is still serving latte and cannolis in the Little Italy neighborhood.

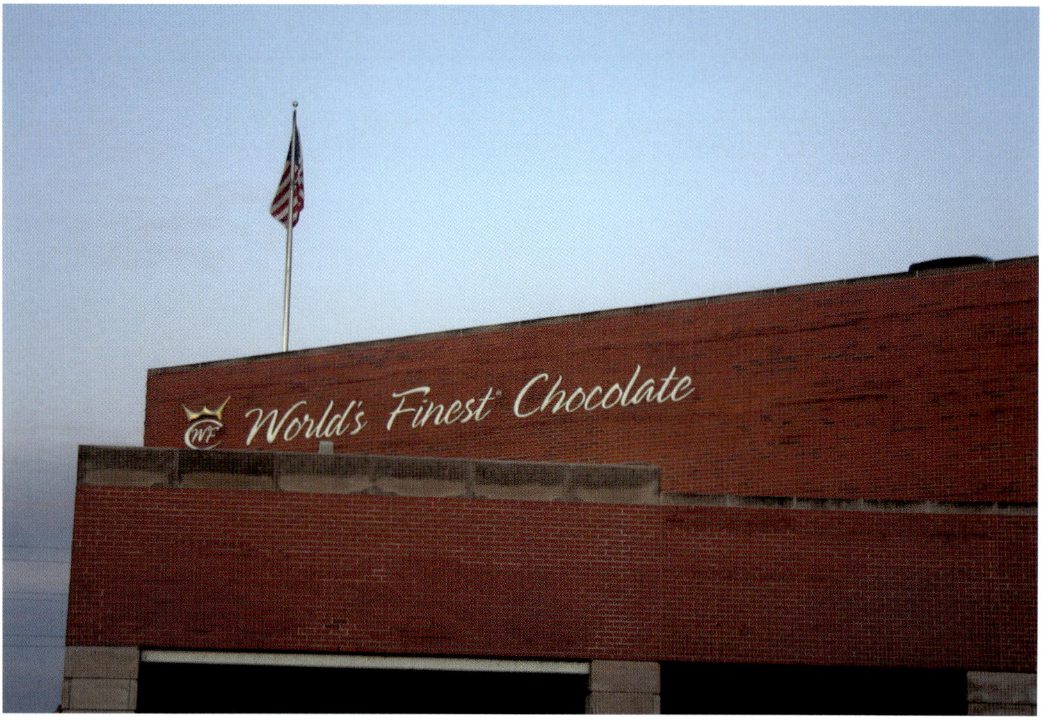

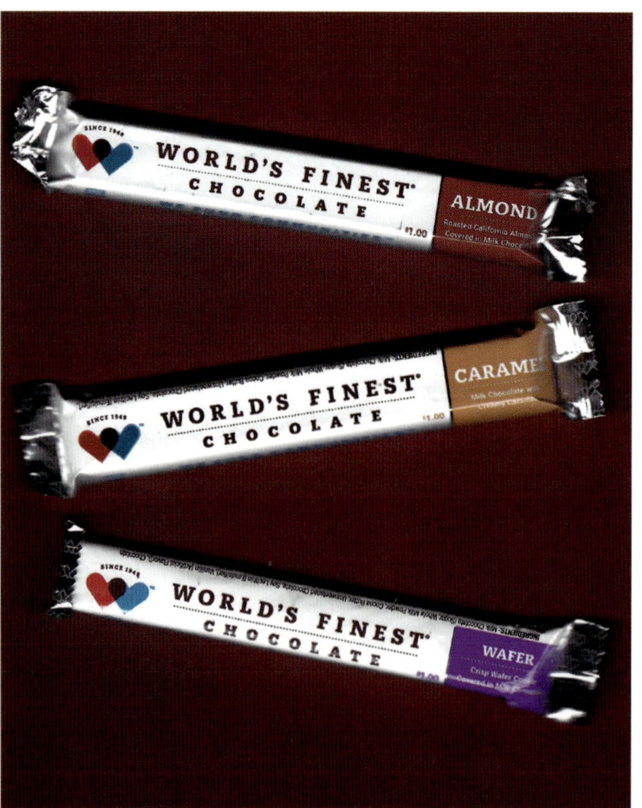

CHOCOLATE CHARITY: The World's Finest Chocolates Company has been productively operating in Chicago for more than seventy years. What sells the candy are the multiple flavors and a zeal for school charitable events.

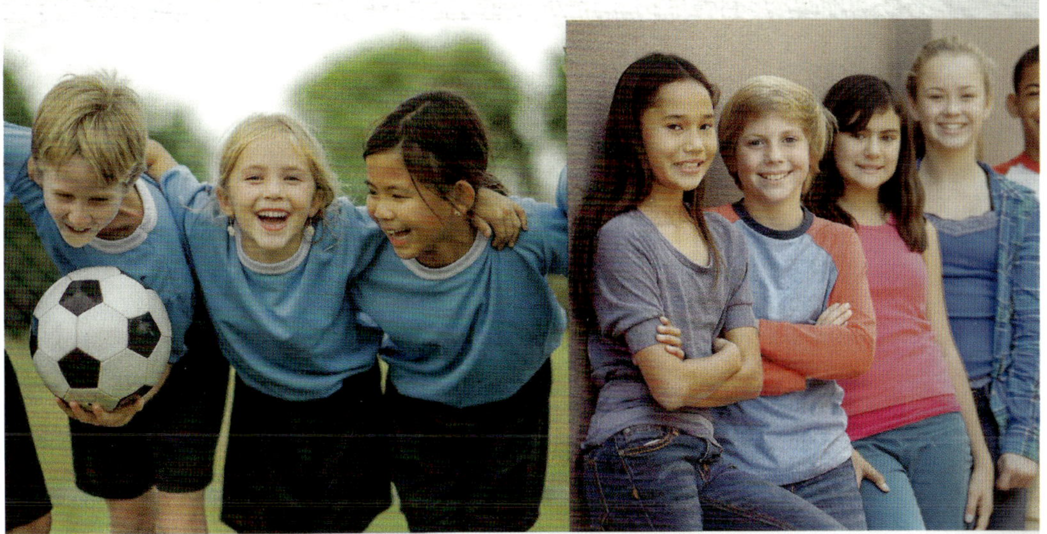

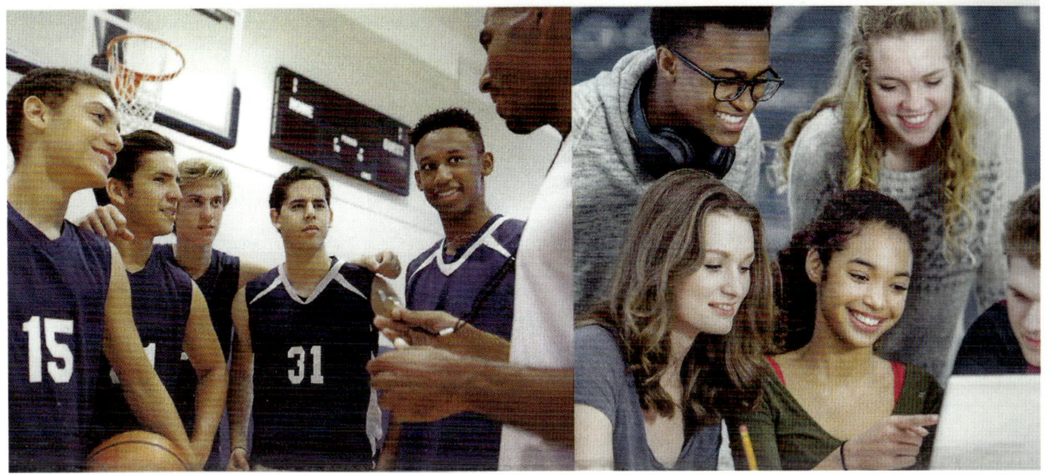

SAVE A SCHOOL: A special feature of the company is providing commercial support for educational institutions. Many schools participate in annual fundraising campaigns powered by students, families, and chocolate bars.

ACKNOWLEDGMENTS

Many historians thrive on past events, places and documents. A book that inspired my research is *Chicago's Southeast Side* by Rod Sellers and Dominic Pacyga. Another inspiration is *Made in Chicago* by Austin Weber. These books taught me that work and industry tell exciting stories.

I am grateful to several institutions in Chicago which hold vast collections on industry and economics. The Chicago Public Library, Harold Washington Branch, is a vital place for general reading and documentation. Visit the library archives and the historic Winter Garden on days when your writing needs a jump start. It will perk you up.

Another important site for planning this book was the Chicago History Museum (CHM), which is a vital source for documents, photographs, and books. For manufacturing references, CHM is a go-to repository.

This book has taken nearly two years to produce. Were it not for friends, history professionals, and family, the book would never be finished. A special note of thanks is due to Kena Longabaugh, Fonthill editor, who has great patience, wisdom, and expertise. I am grateful for her help in publishing this book.

Finally, this book is dedicated to Dr. Byung-In Seo, who not only provided technical advice, but also lent personal support and good faith toward completion.